LLC Wealth Blueprint

Master Your Finances, Maximize Your Growth

By

Nathan Venture, D.

To you,

Thank you!

Table of Contents

Understanding Financial Success for LLC Owners

Running a Limited Liability Company (LLC) presents a unique blend of opportunities and challenges, especially when it comes to managing finances. Financial success for LLC owners isn't just about making money—it's about creating a sustainable, well-managed business that can thrive through ups and downs. This journey requires more than just passion or a solid business idea; it demands strategic financial planning and practical management skills tailored to the distinct structure of an LLC.

LLCs offer flexibility and protection that many entrepreneurs find attractive, but this flexibility can sometimes introduce financial complexity. Owners often juggle multiple hats—manager, investor, accountant—and this can blur the lines between business and personal finances if not handled carefully. Understanding what financial success really means in the context of an LLC is the foundation for making decisions that support your business growth and stability over the long term.

Financial success for LLC owners goes beyond quarterly profits or cash injections. It's about establishing control over your financial destiny, ensuring your business can cover its obligations, invest wisely, and weather unexpected challenges. Achieving this requires a sharp focus on creating a solid financial framework and applying consistent, informed strategies. You'll want to get comfortable with concepts like budgeting, cash flow management, and financial record keeping, but also the less obvious areas such as risk mitigation and profit distribution.

One key element of mastering financial success in an LLC is recognizing the interconnection between your decisions and their financial outcomes. For example, choosing how profits get distributed among members affects tax liabilities and can influence reinvestment in the business. Similarly, having a robust budget system is more than just tracking expenses; it allows you to forecast growth and prepare for investments or lean periods with confidence.

Entrepreneurs who overlook these aspects often find their ventures hampered by avoidable financial struggles. The fast pace of running an LLC can make it tempting to address only immediate needs, but the secret to long-term success lies in deliberate planning paired with disciplined execution. As an LLC owner, setting up a strong financial backbone early can save you from headaches down the road and open doors to opportunities that might otherwise seem out of reach.

Understanding financial success also means appreciating the legal and operational benefits that come with the LLC structure. The limited liability feature protects personal assets from business risks, but it also requires clear separation of business finances from personal ones. This separation not only safeguards your personal finances but also boosts credibility with lenders, investors, and partners. Maintaining transparency and accuracy in your financial dealings is a powerful tool in establishing trust internally and externally.

Moreover, financial success isn't a one-size-fits-all formula. Each LLC is unique in its goals, industry demands, and ownership structure. An owner of a single-member LLC will face different priorities and challenges than members of a multi-member LLC where profit sharing and decision making involve more parties. Recognizing these nuances helps you craft a financial strategy that works best for your particular business model and personal ambitions.

At its core, this book aims to empower you to take control of your LLC's financial health. Equipped with practical tools and knowledge, you'll be able to make decisions grounded in data, reduce uncertainty, and position your LLC to capitalize on growth opportunities. This starts with knowing how to build a sturdy financial foundation, managing cash flow like a pro, understanding tax responsibilities, and much more.

You might wonder why financial literacy is so crucial for an LLC owner amid everything else demanding your time. The answer is simple: your business's financial posture influences every aspect, from day-to-day operations to long-term viability. Without solid financial management, even the most innovative business ideas can falter due to poor cash handling or inadequate planning. Conversely, solid financial practices enable scalability, provide peace of mind, and help you make informed strategic choices that align with your vision.

Another important aspect to consider is the dynamic nature of the business environment. Economic shifts, competitive pressures, and regulatory changes all impact your LLC's finances, often unpredictably. A financially literate owner anticipates these challenges by maintaining agility through contingency planning and sound financial controls. You don't have to predict the future perfectly—but you can prepare for it smartly.

Financial success is also deeply tied to effective use of resources—time, money, and human capital. For example, automating certain financial processes can reduce errors and save valuable time, freeing you up to focus on growing other parts of your business. Leveraging the right technology and understanding financing options can streamline your operations and reduce the stress often associated with managing LLC finances.

Regardless of your experience level, this introduction sets the stage for the detailed guidance you'll find in the chapters ahead. From establishing clear financial goals to navigating tax obligations and financing strategies, you'll discover actionable insights designed for LLC owners who want an edge on managing and growing their enterprises. The chapters will build on this foundation, providing step-by-step approaches tailored to the specific areas that influence financial success.

In essence, understanding financial success for LLC owners is about creating a mindset of intentionality, discipline, and adaptability. It means embracing the numbers alongside the vision and recognizing that financial health forms the backbone of sustainable business growth. With this perspective, you're not just managing a business—you're building a legacy that can endure and thrive.

Chapter 1: Building a Strong Financial Foundation for Your LLC

Establishing a solid financial foundation is the backbone of any successful LLC, providing the stability needed to grow and adapt over time. This starts with clarity about what your business aims to achieve financially and the discipline to implement systems that support those goals consistently. Without a strong base, challenges like unpredictable expenses or missed opportunities can quickly derail progress. By focusing early on building sound financial habits—such as disciplined budgeting and goal-setting—you create a roadmap that guides daily decisions and long-term strategies, empowering you to navigate uncertainties with confidence. The process demands attention and commitment, but the payoff is a business that not only survives but thrives in today's competitive market.

Setting Clear Financial Goals for Your LLC

Setting clear financial goals is the foundation upon which your LLC's financial success will be built. Without well-defined objectives, it's easy to drift aimlessly in terms of expenses, investments, and growth strategies. Financial goals give your business direction, help prioritize resources, and provide measurable milestones to celebrate or adjust your approach. For entrepreneurs and small business owners, these goals are not just numbers on a page—they are critical tools that guide decision-making and inspire focus amid the many daily demands of running an LLC.

The first step in setting financial goals for your LLC is to distinguish between short-term and long-term targets. Short-term goals might include achieving a certain monthly revenue, maintaining a minimum cash reserve, or reducing specific operating costs within the next quarter. These smaller objectives keep your day-to-day operations aligned and help you make continuous progress. Long-term goals, on the other hand, often relate to scaling the company, such as expanding into new markets, reaching a set annual revenue milestone, or preparing for an eventual exit strategy. Balancing these horizons is essential; without short-term wins, long-term visions remain unrealistic, and without long-term goals, day-to-day efforts can feel scattered or lack motivation.

Another critical factor to consider when setting your LLC's financial goals is specificity. Vague goals like "grow revenue" or "increase profits" don't provide enough clarity to act upon or measure. Instead, aim for goals that are clear and quantifiable. For example, "Increase monthly recurring revenue by 20% within twelve months" or "Reduce monthly overhead expenses by 10% within six months." These specific targets allow you to track progress objectively and make informed adjustments when results don't align with expectations.

One challenge many LLC owners face is setting goals that are either too ambitious or too conservative. Goals that are unattainably high can be demoralizing and may lead to burnout or strategic missteps. Goals set too low might result in missed opportunities and stagnation. Striking the right balance requires a realistic assessment of your current financial position, industry benchmarks, and potential market conditions. Conducting thorough research and, when possible, consulting with financial advisors or mentors can provide a valuable reality check that keeps your goals challenging yet achievable.

Equally important is aligning financial goals with your overall business mission and values. Financial success doesn't exist in a vacuum—it supports your broader vision, whether that's creating innovative products, providing excellent service, or ensuring sustainable community impact. When your financial objectives resonate with your personal and organizational values, motivation remains high, and decision-making naturally centers on what matters most to your LLC.

Setting goals also involves prioritization. Your LLC might have multiple financial targets, but not all can take precedence simultaneously. Prioritize based on urgency, impact, and resource availability. For example, securing positive cash flow might be more critical initially than aggressive expansion. As your business stabilizes and resources free up, larger growth goals become attainable. This staged approach helps avoid spreading your efforts too thin and ensures steady, consistent progress.

One way to improve goal-setting discipline is to incorporate the SMART criteria: goals should be Specific, Measurable, Achievable, Relevant, and Time-bound. This framework ensures your goals have clear definitions, timelines for achievement, and are relevant to your business context. Let's break down how SMART works for an LLC owner:

1. **Specific**: Your goal should clearly state what you want to accomplish. For example, "Increase storefront sales by 15%" rather than just "Increase sales."

2. **Measurable**: Without measurable criteria, you can't track progress. Using sales percentage improvement, profit margins, or customer acquisition numbers are all measurable metrics.

3. **Achievable**: Set realistic goals based on your business capacity, market conditions, and current trends to avoid setting yourself up for failure.
4. **Relevant**: Goals must align with your broader business objectives and mission to maintain coherence in your strategy.
5. **Time-bound**: Setting a deadline creates focus and urgency, helping prevent procrastination and ensuring accountability.

Equipped with SMART goals, LLC owners find it easier to communicate financial expectations to their teams, investors, or partners. Clear targets foster a shared understanding of what success looks like, making collaboration more productive and reducing misalignments that might cause costly errors.

Additionally, regularly revisiting and revising your financial goals is crucial. Businesses evolve, market conditions change, and sometimes unexpected hurdles demand flexibility. Scheduling periodic reviews—whether quarterly or biannually—means you can evaluate whether your goals remain realistic and aligned with your business's current trajectory. During these check-ins, analyze what's working, what isn't, and decide if you need to pivot your financial objectives or strategies accordingly.

It's also worth mentioning that financial goal-setting isn't just about revenue or profit; cash flow is equally important. Many LLCs fail not because they aren't growing revenue, but because they don't manage cash flow effectively. Setting specific cash flow goals—like maintaining a minimum cash balance to cover expenses for three months—can prevent crises and provide peace of mind. Such buffer goals are often overlooked but essential for stability and resilience.

Another aspect that can provide motivation and clarity involves linking financial goals to personal aspirations. If you're operating your LLC to achieve lifestyle flexibility, financial independence, or to create generational wealth, ensuring your business goals reflect these ambitions is vital. When your financial targets support your personal purpose, you build resilience that helps you push through tough times and stay committed over the long haul.

Sometimes, LLC owners hesitate to set detailed financial goals due to fear of failure or uncertainty. However, goals don't have to be a source of stress—they should be your tools for empowerment. Even if you miss a target, what matters is learning from the experience and refining your approach. The clarity you gain through goal-setting offers better control over your financial future and fosters confidence in your decisions.

Finally, sharing your financial goals with trusted advisors or mentors can multiply their effectiveness. External insights can help identify blind spots, suggest opportunities you didn't consider, and hold you accountable. Accountability partners create an additional layer of motivation to work toward your goals consistently and thoughtfully.

In summary, setting clear financial goals for your LLC means defining what you want to achieve in specific, measurable, and timely ways. Align these goals with your business vision and personal values while keeping them realistic and flexible. Prioritize your objectives to maintain focus and revisit them regularly to adapt as needed. When done well, this practice transforms your financial planning from guesswork into a purposeful roadmap driving your LLC toward long-term success.

Establishing a Reliable Budgeting System for Your LLC

Creating and maintaining a solid budgeting system is fundamental for any LLC aiming to build a strong financial foundation. Without a budget, it's nearly impossible to understand where your money is going or to make informed decisions that drive growth. A reliable budgeting system acts as a financial blueprint, helping you allocate resources wisely, control expenses, and prepare for the unexpected. It also enables you to measure performance and adapt your strategies as your business evolves.

At its core, a budget is more than just a list of numbers. It's a dynamic tool that reflects your LLC's financial goals while providing a clear picture of daily operations and future projections. Setting up a dependable budgeting system means capturing accurate income forecasts, fixed and variable expenses, and identifying key financial indicators that affect your business. The act of budgeting compels you to anticipate revenue fluctuations and assign funds accordingly, which reduces the risk of cash shortfalls.

One challenge many entrepreneurs face when budgeting for their LLC is the temptation to create overly optimistic revenue estimates. While aiming high can be motivating, an unrealistic budget may quickly become a source of frustration and poor decision-making. A trustworthy budgeting system requires disciplined, conservative estimates grounded in actual historical data and market research. Starting with realistic baseline assumptions lays the groundwork for a budget you can rely on and adjust pragmatically.

Developing your budgeting system also involves deciding how detailed you want your budget to be. Some LLC owners prefer broad categories—like marketing, payroll, and supplies—while others break those down into more granular line items. The right choice depends on the size of your LLC and the complexity of its operations. Smaller LLCs might benefit from simpler budgets that save time, while larger ones or those with multiple revenue streams often need a more intricate approach to avoid blind spots in financial management.

Technology plays a crucial role in establishing and managing your budget effectively. There are numerous budgeting and accounting software solutions tailored to small businesses and LLCs, offering features like automatic expense tracking, real-time updates, and customizable reports. Integrating these tools into your budgeting system adds accuracy, reduces manual errors, and ultimately saves valuable time. It's important not to overlook the utility of such software; the right digital tools can transform a daunting budgeting task into an insightful and manageable process.

Tracking expenses consistently is a cornerstone of any reliable budgeting system. This means regular recording of all costs, both fixed and variable, ensures your budget reflects actual spending rather than perceived or estimated amounts. Many LLCs struggle when expenses sneak past unnoticed—like small subscription fees, minor office supplies, or occasional contractor costs—that cumulatively impact the bottom line. When your budget system is set up to capture every dollar going out, you can identify patterns, adjust spending, and allocate resources more strategically.

Another important aspect is budgeting for irregular or unexpected expenses. Unlike a paycheck or predictable monthly bills, LLCs often face periodic costs such as equipment repairs, legal fees, or seasonal inventory purchases. Your system should include a contingency fund or allowance within the budget to absorb these unpredictable hits. Incorporating this buffer improves your financial resilience and prevents emergency expenses from derailing your operations.

Budget reviews should be part of your ongoing financial routine. Setting a monthly or quarterly cadence for revisiting your budget allows you to compare actual results against projections. This comparison reveals variances that require analysis and course correction. Left unchecked, variances can erode profit margins or cause cash flow issues. A disciplined review process encourages accountability and encourages smarter financial decisions based on data rather than guesswork.

It's not uncommon for LLC owners to feel overwhelmed when first setting up a budgeting system. However, the complexity of your budget can evolve. Starting simple with core income and expense categories is perfectly acceptable—and often advisable. You can add layers of detail as your understanding improves and as your business needs grow. The goal is to create a sustainable habit of tracking and controlling finances rather than a perfect document on day one.

Engaging your LLC team, if you have one, in the budgeting process is another strategy to enhance your system's reliability. When everyone understands the budget goals and limitations, it helps foster a culture of financial responsibility throughout the company. Team members can alert you to overlooked expenses or savings opportunities, and collective ownership of the budget strengthens commitment to sticking with it.

A well-established budgeting system directly supports other key financial strategies you'll employ as an LLC owner. For instance, it feeds vital data into your cash flow management, tax planning, and investment decisions. Each of those areas depends on clear visibility into your financial priorities and performance. Through budget discipline, you gain confidence in allocating capital toward growth initiatives, managing debt wisely, and funding operational improvements.

Many successful entrepreneurs advise treating your budget like a living document—one that grows and adapts alongside your business. Economic environments shift, your LLC's goals evolve, and unexpected challenges arise. Rigidity in budgeting leads to missed opportunities or financial strain, while flexibility allows you to respond strategically. Revising your budget proactively, rather than reactively, keeps your financial foundation solid and aligned with your vision.

Lastly, take care not to allow budgeting to become a dreaded chore. Setting aside regular, manageable blocks of time to update and analyze your budget ensures it doesn't pile up or become an afterthought. The more routine you make this practice, the more natural it feels—and the greater the impact on your LLC's financial health. Over time, budgeting transforms from a task to a powerful driver of business success.

Chapter 2: Mastering Cash Flow Management in LLCs

Managing cash flow is the lifeblood of any LLC, and mastering it means your business stays resilient through both feast and famine. It's not just about tracking what's coming in and going out, but anticipating cash needs before they become emergencies, allowing you to make smarter decisions that keep operations smooth and growth steady. By establishing a proactive approach to cash flow, you'll avoid the pitfalls of delayed payments, unexpected expenses, or missed opportunities that can derail progress. This chapter will guide you to gain control over your LLC's financial rhythm so you're never caught off guard, empowering you to maintain stability, invest wisely, and build a thriving business with confidence.

Tracking and Forecasting Cash Flow for LLC Stability

One of the most critical factors that can make or break an LLC is cash flow management. Without a clear picture of how money moves in and out of the business, it's nearly impossible to maintain stability, let alone plan for growth. Tracking and forecasting cash flow are the foundational tools that give you insight into your LLC's financial health. They allow you to anticipate periods of surplus and shortage, prepare for upcoming expenses, and make informed decisions based on reliable data rather than guesswork.

Tracking cash flow means diligently monitoring every dollar that enters or leaves your LLC's accounts. It requires more than just noting sales and expenses; it involves breaking down income sources, payment timings, and expense categories. Tracking isn't a one-time action but a continuous process that reveals patterns over weeks, months, or quarters. When you track cash flow regularly, you uncover fluctuations that can point to seasonal trends, customer payment behaviors, or operational inefficiencies. This ongoing visibility is invaluable—it helps you avoid nasty surprises like unexpected overdrafts and missed opportunities to invest excess cash wisely.

For many LLC owners, the complexity of tracking cash flow seems daunting at first, but it doesn't have to be. Establish a simple, consistent system that fits your business's scale and complexity. If you use accounting software, leverage its cash flow tracking features to generate reports that detail inflows and outflows over selected periods. For those preferring manual methods, maintain ledgers or spreadsheets that record all transactions categorized by type and timing. However you do it, the goal is to develop a methodical and repeatable practice that captures data accurately and on time.

Once you have solid cash flow data, forecasting becomes the next essential step. Forecasting projects future cash inflows and outflows based on historical patterns, current contracts, and anticipated expenses. It's about looking ahead to understand the financial runway your LLC has at any given moment. Forecasting cash flow can be done weekly, monthly, or quarterly depending on the volatility and needs of your business. Frequent forecasting helps you identify when you might face cash shortages or surpluses before they occur, giving you time to plan accordingly.

There's a huge advantage in combining both short-term and long-term forecasting. On the short-term side, you focus on immediate needs such as payroll, supplier payments, or upcoming client billings.

Long-term forecasts take a broader view, including anticipated growth, capital expenditures, and potential funding rounds. Both perspectives are necessary for maintaining LLC stability. Short-term forecasts prevent operational hiccups caused by cash crunches, while long-term forecasts guide strategic decisions like hiring, launching new products, or entering partnerships.

Forecasting isn't about achieving perfect accuracy—it's about informed estimation to make smarter choices. Some variables will always remain unpredictable, like sudden client cancellations or unexpected expenses. Providing flexibility in your cash flow model allows you to adjust forecasts regularly as real-world data comes in. Remember, a forecast that is revisited and refined frequently becomes a powerful tool to keep your business adaptive and resilient.

One effective way to enhance your cash flow tracking and forecasting is to focus on your accounts receivable and payable. Knowing exactly when payments are expected from clients and when bills need to be paid is critical. Late or delayed payments can cause unexpected cash shortages, so establishing clear payment terms and following up on unpaid invoices promptly can make a considerable difference. On the other hand, negotiating favorable payment terms with suppliers—such as extended due dates—can help ease cash flow pressures.

Tracking and forecasting also require you to keep an eye on non-operational cash movements. This includes loan payments, owner draws, and any unexpected one-time expenses. Ignoring these can cause your forecasts to be misleading or overly optimistic. Build a comprehensive picture of every financial activity affecting your cash position. The more complete your data, the more trustworthy your forecasts will be.

While manual tracking and forecasting techniques can work, many LLC owners benefit from using specialized financial tools. Software designed for small businesses and LLCs can automate data collection, categorize transactions, and generate real-time cash flow reports. These applications can also simulate different cash flow scenarios, helping you evaluate the potential impact of new contracts, expenses, or loan repayments. However, remember that technology is only as effective as the input it receives—consistent data entry and review remain essential.

Another practical tip is to establish key performance indicators (KPIs) related to cash flow. Metrics like days sales outstanding (DSO), cash conversion cycle, and liquidity ratios can offer insights into how efficiently your LLC is converting sales into cash and managing its financial obligations. Monitoring these KPIs over time allows you to spot troublesome trends quickly and take corrective action well before cash flow issues threaten your stability.

Beyond using tools and metrics, communicating your cash flow status regularly with all stakeholders involved in the LLC is vital. Whether it's partners, investors, or managers, everyone should be aligned on cash availability and constraints. Transparent discussions about cash flow foster trust and joint problem-solving when challenges arise. By keeping communication channels open, you can also leverage collective expertise to optimize cash management strategies effectively.

Ultimately, tracking and forecasting cash flow forms the backbone of financial discipline in LLCs. Without these practices, your business may survive in the short term but struggle to sustain itself through inevitable ups and downs. Embracing these processes enables you to maintain stability, plan proactively, and seize growth opportunities with confidence. A stable cash flow foundation frees you from constant firefighting around finances and shifts your focus to steering your LLC toward long-term success.

It's important to recognize that building a reliable cash flow tracking and forecasting system takes time and practice. You won't get it perfect from day one, but consistent effort will pay off. Start by setting up simple tracking mechanisms, then gradually enhance them with forecasting layers and automation. Make reviewing your cash flow a non-negotiable part of your routine. This habit becomes a powerful advantage, allowing your LLC to respond swiftly to changes in market conditions, client behavior, or operational shifts.

In summary, mastering cash flow stability for your LLC hinges on two key actions: careful tracking and thoughtful forecasting. They provide clarity on your financial position, enhance decision-making, and reduce risk. By transforming raw financial data into actionable insights, your LLC can stay solvent during challenging periods and capitalize on growth phases without unnecessary stress. As an LLC owner, your commitment to these financial management practices positions your business for both immediate stability and future prosperity.

Strategies to Optimize LLC Cash Flow in Real Time

One of the most crucial aspects of running an LLC successfully is managing cash flow effectively—not just in hindsight, but in real time. Cash flow isn't a static number; it fluctuates constantly with sales, expenses, and unforeseen events. The ability to optimize your LLC's cash flow as these changes happen can be the difference between thriving and struggling. To put it simply, optimizing cash flow in real time means staying ahead of the curve so that your business never runs out of the funds needed for day-to-day operations, investments, or emergency needs.

Real-time cash flow management starts with gaining immediate insight into the money moving in and out of your business. Modern financial technologies have made this much more accessible than in the past. Cash flow optimization is no longer about waiting for the end-of-month reports or quarterly financial statements. Instead, it's about leveraging tools and strategies that give LLC owners up-to-the-minute visibility into their financial position—and using that information to make fast, informed decisions.

First, establish a system that allows constant monitoring of your incoming revenue streams alongside your outgoing expenses. This might mean connecting your accounting software directly to your bank accounts, so transactions update automatically. When transactions appear in real time, you can quickly spot cash inflow delays or unexpected expenditures and respond accordingly—whether that's by accelerating collections, postponing discretionary spending, or tapping into short-term financing. Without this immediate awareness, decision-making becomes reactive rather than proactive.

Another key strategy is prioritizing your accounts receivable management. Late payments are one of the biggest threats to an LLC's cash flow. If customers consistently pay late, the strain on your working capital can be severe. Implementing clear payment terms upfront and following up with gentle but firm reminders as due dates approach assures steadier cash inflows. Many businesses benefit from offering early payment discounts or implementing online payment portals to simplify and speed up collections. The more efficient your receivables are, the less you have to worry about cash crunches emerging unexpectedly.

On the flip side, managing accounts payable with a strategic mindset is equally important. While it's tempting to delay payments to conserve cash, it's vital to balance that with maintaining good relationships with suppliers and avoiding late fees. One effective approach is negotiating payment terms with vendors that align better with your cash cycle—for example, extending payment windows when revenue is slow or syncing payment dates to follow your own customer payment schedules. Having this fluidity gives your LLC breathing room to navigate tight moments without risking disruptions in supply or service.

Cash flow optimization isn't simply about cutting costs, though controlling expenses plays a role. Consider implementing variable cost structures where feasible, so that spending aligns more closely with revenue levels. Fixed expenses can tie up valuable cash unnecessarily during lulls. On the other hand, scalable costs, such as contract-based services or temporary staffing, allow flexibility that can protect your cash position. In times where real-time data indicates an impending cash shortage, scaling back certain expenses quickly and temporarily can help maintain liquidity.

The timing of cash flow is another lever that savvy LLC owners use to their advantage. Not all cash inflows and outflows occur at convenient intervals, but you can optimize these timings. For instance, scheduling large-payments-in or large-expenses-out at moments when cash reserves are abundant ensures your company won't face shortages. Similarly, making partial payments or splitting larger expenses over multiple periods can help smooth out cash outflows. The goal is to create a more balanced cash flow rhythm rather than having wild spikes and drops that may catch you off guard.

Using cash flow forecasting as a live, dynamic process also goes hand-in-hand with real-time optimization. While the previous section explored forecasting as a foundational technique, it's important here to think of forecasts as living tools that you update frequently with new data. Adjust your predictions based on recent sales trends, payment behaviors, or unexpected expenses as they happen. Doing this regularly lets your team recognize potential shortfalls days or weeks in advance and deploy strategic fixes proactively, avoiding crises.

Automation can dramatically improve the effectiveness of real-time cash flow strategies. Accounting platforms now allow customization that triggers alerts when cash balances fall below a set threshold or when invoices remain unpaid past their due date. These automated notifications act like guardrails, prompting you to investigate issues immediately rather than discovering them too late. In some cases, automatic electronic payments can even be timed to optimize cash balances, ensuring you avoid overdrafts or missed payments without constant manual oversight.

Beyond technology, maintaining clear financial communication within your LLC's leadership is essential. When cash flow challenges arise, having open, fact-based discussions with partners or key employees helps generate timely solutions and fosters a culture of fiscal responsibility. Everyone involved should understand how their roles impact cash flow, from sales and customer service to procurement and operations. This collective awareness creates a faster and more coordinated response to cash flow issues, minimizing disruption to your LLC's growth.

Another useful tactic when managing cash flow in real time is to build contingency plans for common pitfalls. For example, you might maintain a dedicated line of credit or reserve fund that you can tap without delay when cash runs low unexpectedly. Having these buffers ready means you can address shortfalls instantly rather than scrambling under pressure. Preparing these safety nets ahead of time changes your cash flow optimization from simply reactive to strongly proactive.

At its heart, optimizing cash flow in real time is about fostering agility within your LLC's financial operations. This agility depends partly on access to accurate, instant data and partly on creating policies and processes that empower you to act quickly. Flexibility in how you manage receivables, payables, expenses, and cash reserves gives you the freedom to navigate everyday uncertainties without jeopardizing your business health.

Lastly, never underestimate the power of regular financial reviews. While "real time" suggests looking at cash flow moment by moment, it's also critical to pause periodically—daily, weekly, or biweekly—to analyze what the numbers are telling you beyond the surface. This reflection helps identify recurring patterns or inefficiencies you can address systematically, rather than repeatedly responding to symptoms.

Through consistent attention and strategic adjustments, you'll transform cash flow management from a source of stress into a competitive advantage for your LLC. When you master cash flow in real time, you build the foundation that supports sustainable growth and financial resilience, positioning your business for success no matter what challenges come your way.

Chapter 3: Navigating LLC Tax Responsibilities

Understanding how taxes affect your LLC can feel overwhelming, but it's a crucial step to keep your business compliant and financially healthy. Taxes for LLCs vary depending on your state and the federal rules applicable to your business type, so staying informed and organized is key. By proactively managing your tax obligations, you avoid costly penalties and open the door to maximizing savings through available deductions and credits. This chapter lays the foundation for grasping the essentials of your LLC's tax responsibilities, empowering you to make confident decisions that keep your finances on track and your business positioned for growth.

Understanding Federal and State Taxes for LLCs

When it comes to running a limited liability company (LLC), understanding how federal and state taxes work is absolutely critical. LLCs offer a lot of flexibility when it comes to taxation, but with that flexibility comes some complexity. Unlike corporations, LLCs aren't inherently taxed as entities; instead, they often pass their income through to their owners, who then pay taxes on their personal returns. However, the story doesn't end there. The way the IRS and individual states treat LLCs can vary significantly, and if you don't get a solid grasp on these differences, you could be facing unexpected tax bills or penalties.

One key point to remember is that an LLC is considered a "pass-through" entity for federal tax purposes by default. This means that the company itself doesn't pay income tax. Instead, profits and losses flow through to the members, who then report them on their personal income tax returns. If you're a single-member LLC, this usually means filing a Schedule C along with your Form 1040, while multi-member LLCs typically file Form 1065, and members receive K-1s detailing their share of income and expenses. This setup avoids the "double taxation" that corporations often face, where both the business and the shareholders are taxed.

But don't confuse the default treatment for the only option. LLCs can elect to be taxed differently by filing specific forms with the IRS. For instance, an LLC can choose to be taxed as an S corporation or a C corporation. These elections depend on your business goals, income level, and other financial considerations. Such decisions can greatly impact how much tax you pay, what kind of returns you need to file, and even how you pay yourself as a business owner.

Aside from federal taxation, state taxes can make this landscape more complicated. Every state has its own rules and rates when it comes to taxing LLCs, and this can include income taxes, franchise taxes, gross receipts taxes, or some combination of these. For example, some states impose a franchise tax based on an LLC's net worth or capital, while others might charge a fee simply for operating in the state. Knowing your state's requirements upfront isn't just smart— it's essential to avoid surprises down the road.

In many states, LLC owners must also consider state income tax obligations. Usually, members report their shares of income on their individual state tax returns. But there are exceptions. Some states don't tax personal income, which can be a major advantage if your LLC is based there. Others require the LLC itself to pay an income tax or an alternative minimum tax, even if the federal government treats it as pass-through income. Understanding these nuances allows you to factor state taxes into your overall tax planning strategy properly.

The complexity increases when your LLC operates in multiple states. In that situation, you need to determine where your business has "nexus," or a significant presence. Nexus rules vary widely but generally depend on factors like having physical locations, employees, or generating substantial revenue within a state's borders. Without properly apportioning income between states where you operate, you risk underpaying or overpaying taxes, both of which can be costly and trigger audits.

Another common pain point for LLC owners is self-employment tax. Since LLC income typically passes through to members as ordinary income, it's usually subject to self-employment tax in addition to federal income tax. This covers Social Security and Medicare taxes, which traditional employees split with employers. For LLC owners, the entire amount often falls on them. This is something that can catch people off guard if they don't plan ahead, so working with an accountant who understands how to calculate and potentially reduce self-employment tax is well worth the investment.

For those LLCs that elect S corporation taxation, self-employment tax treatment shifts somewhat. Owners may pay themselves a reasonable salary (which is subject to payroll taxes) and take additional profits as distributions that are not subject to self-employment tax. But there's a delicate balance here. The IRS watches these arrangements closely to ensure owners aren't underpaying payroll taxes by taking unreasonably low salaries. Correctly structuring your compensation is both a tax and compliance necessity.

It's also worth mentioning that LLCs aren't always exempt from sales tax. If your business sells goods or certain services, you might need to register to collect and remit sales tax in your state or states where you do business. Sales tax laws are notoriously complex and vary not just by state, but sometimes by locality within the state. Failing to collect or report sales taxes properly can lead to fines and penalties. While this doesn't fall under income taxation, it is a critical piece of the overall tax puzzle that LLC owners must navigate.

Payroll taxes are another consideration for LLCs with employees. Even if your LLC is a pass-through entity for income tax purposes, you're still responsible for withholding and remitting payroll taxes like federal and state income tax withholding, Social Security, Medicare, and unemployment tax. Setting up the right payroll system and staying current on tax law changes can make a world of difference in managing these responsibilities efficiently.

Tax deadlines are often overlooked but missing them can be costly. Federal income taxes for LLC members generally follow the calendar for individual returns, but the LLC itself may have filing requirements such as Form 1065 due by March 15 for multi-member LLCs. State deadlines vary significantly, so it pays to be proactive. Creating a tax calendar that tracks all federal, state, and local filing dates keeps things on track and avoids penalties and interest for late payments.

Documentation is a subtle but powerful part of managing your LLC taxes. Maintaining clear, organized records of your income, expenses, payroll, and distributions not only supports accurate tax filings but also reduces the stress when it's time to file or if you face an audit. Using accounting software tailored to LLC needs can simplify this task, ensuring you're capturing everything your tax preparer needs and securing your financial health for the long term.

One motivator for diving deep into understanding federal and state taxes is the potential to keep more of what your LLC earns. Tax laws offer various credits, deductions, and incentives that, when properly utilized, can significantly lower your tax burden. Some of these will be covered later in more detail, but know upfront that every dollar you save in taxes is a dollar you can reinvest in your business or use to grow your personal wealth.

Finally, staying informed and seeking professional guidance can transform tax compliance from a dreaded chore into a strategic advantage. Tax laws change frequently, and what worked last year might not apply today. Establishing a relationship with a tax professional familiar with LLCs can provide tailored advice and timely updates. It's an investment in peace of mind and in securing your LLC's financial future.

In conclusion, understanding federal and state taxes is no small feat, but it's one of the most important responsibilities you carry as an LLC owner. The tax choices you make influence how much you pay, how you report income, and how you plan for growth. By mastering this knowledge, you position your LLC not just to comply, but to thrive financially, minimizing surprises and maximizing opportunities every tax season.

Leveraging Tax Deductions and Credits Specifically for LLCs

When you own or operate an LLC, understanding how to leverage tax deductions and credits is crucial for maximizing your profitability and staying compliant. LLCs bring unique tax considerations compared to other business structures, and tapping into available deductions and credits can significantly lower your overall tax burden. Too often, business owners either overlook or underutilize these opportunities, losing out on savings that could be reinvested into growth or stabilize cash flow during lean periods.

The first step in leveraging tax deductions is recognizing that LLCs have flexibility in how they're taxed. Depending on your LLC's election, you might be treated as a sole proprietorship, partnership, S corporation, or even C corporation for tax purposes. That flexibility means your deductible expenses can vary, but some deductions commonly apply across many LLCs. These deductions directly reduce the amount of taxable income, which in turn lowers the taxes owed. Conversely, tax credits reduce taxes dollar for dollar, offering even greater savings when applicable. Solid knowledge of both gives you a dual advantage in managing your LLC's effective tax rate.

One common and often significant deduction for LLCs is the business use of home. If you operate your LLC from home, either partially or entirely, you may qualify to deduct a reasonable percentage of your rent or mortgage interest, utilities, insurance, and maintenance costs. The key lies in accurately calculating the portion of your home dedicated exclusively to business activities, and being diligent about documentation. Properly claiming this deduction can save a substantial amount annually, but be mindful of IRS rules to avoid audits or penalties.

Another major category includes vehicle expenses. If you or your employees regularly use a car for LLC business operations, you can deduct costs related to fuel, maintenance, insurance, lease payments, and depreciation. Business mileage records must be thorough and precise, so keeping a mileage log is indispensable. The IRS offers a standard mileage rate option, which simplifies calculations but might not always be as advantageous as deducting actual expenses, especially if your vehicle is expensive or heavily used for business. Weighing both methods each tax year can prevent missed opportunities.

LLCs with employees have additional deductible items like wages, payroll taxes, and benefits. Not only do these deductions reduce your taxable income, but offering competitive benefits can have the dual effect of retaining talent and improving company culture. Beyond basics like salary, voluntary retirement plans, health insurance premiums, and even employee education programs qualify as deductible business expenses. Leveraging these can create a win-win situation for business growth and tax efficiency simultaneously.

Purchases of equipment, software, and other assets necessary for LLC operations also offer valuable tax reduction opportunities. The Section 179 deduction, for example, allows LLCs to expense the full cost of qualifying property in the year it was placed in service rather than spreading the expense out over several years. This immediate write-off accelerates tax benefits, which can be especially helpful for startups or growing businesses investing heavily in technology, machinery, or office furniture. Making sure to track assets accurately and properly classify expenses is essential to avoid complications or disallowed claims.

In addition to deductions, tax credits specifically available for LLCs can sometimes provide a direct dollar-for-dollar reduction of the tax owed, which is even more valuable than a simple deduction. Credits vary widely based on business activities and locations but may include options such as the research and development (R&D) credit, energy efficiency credits, or small employer health insurance credits. Qualifying for credits often requires meeting particular criteria, so understanding the eligibility rules and maintaining solid records makes all the difference.

For example, if your LLC invests in renewable energy or energy-efficient equipment, you could unlock significant federal or state credits. These types of incentives not only help reduce tax bills but also promote sustainable business models—a growing priority for customers and communities alike. Similarly, small LLCs providing health insurance to employees might qualify for a health coverage tax credit, lowering the cost of offering these essential benefits. Actively seeking out such credits rather than waiting for your accountant to mention them usually pays off handsomely.

Another strategic approach involves timing expenses to maximize deductions and credits. Since LLCs typically report taxes on a calendar or fiscal year, carefully planning when to incur business expenses or make investments can influence which tax year you'll benefit from the deductions. Delaying certain purchases until after the new tax year or accelerating expenses by year-end are common strategies. However, these must align with your cash flow realities and growth objectives to avoid financial strain.

It's also important to consider the interplay between state and federal tax incentives. Some deductions and credits available at the federal level might be limited or nonexistent in your state, while others could be exclusively offered by state governments. Each state has its own tax laws and programs designed to encourage local business development, so research—ideally with professional assistance—to uncover these can add meaningful savings. For LLC owners working across multiple states, the complexity increases, but with careful planning, you can avoid paying redundant taxes or miss out on state-specific incentives.

Many LLC owners find it useful to develop a proactive tax strategy for each fiscal year that incorporates a review of both deductions and credits available. This helps ensure no opportunity slips through the cracks as the business evolves. Having an ongoing relationship with a knowledgeable accountant or tax advisor who understands the nuances of LLC taxation can make a huge difference. Their guidance can identify lesser-known deductions or emerging credits tailored to your industry, keeping you ahead of the curve.

One example includes the qualified business income (QBI) deduction introduced by tax reform legislation. This deduction allows eligible LLC taxpayers to deduct up to 20% of their qualified business income from pass-through entities. Although the rules can get complex depending on your income level and business type, this deduction represents one of the largest tax benefits an LLC can leverage. Many entrepreneurs miss out on it due to misunderstandings or lack of proper preparation, so investing time to understand its criteria and documentation requirements pays big dividends.

Health savings accounts (HSAs) and retirement plans also offer potential tax advantages worth integrating into your LLC's overall deductions framework. Contributions to these accounts can be deducted at the business level, and benefits to employees enhance your company's attractiveness without excessive cost. These elements not only support your team but also reduce taxable income, boosting the LLC's financial health. Mapping out a long-term benefits strategy aligned with tax-efficient tools can strengthen your business for years to come.

Finally, recordkeeping cannot be overstated in importance. Accurate and organized documentation of every expense, invoice, mileage log, benefit plan, and investment ensures you can substantiate deductions and credits if ever audited. Automated bookkeeping systems tailored for LLCs are increasingly affordable and user-friendly, providing real-time insights while reducing human error. Establishing a consistent habit of tracking tax-related items throughout the year removes year-end stress and positions your LLC for maximum advantage.

Ultimately, leveraging tax deductions and credits for your LLC is more than just a tax-season exercise—it's a form of strategic financial management that can fuel growth, improve profitability, and enhance your competitive edge. By understanding the most relevant deductions, exploring applicable credits, and maintaining disciplined recordkeeping, you build a foundation that empowers your LLC to thrive. The more proactive and informed you are in leveraging these tools, the closer you get to mastering your financial future as a successful LLC owner.

Chapter 4: Strategic Investment Planning for LLC Growth

To fuel the expansion of your LLC, strategic investment planning is essential—it's not just about throwing money at opportunities but making calculated decisions that align with your long-term vision. You need to evaluate where your capital will generate the greatest impact while considering the nature of your business, market conditions, and growth objectives. Balancing risk with potential returns requires a clear understanding of which investments complement your core operations and which might expose you to unnecessary volatility. Thoughtful planning ensures you use your resources efficiently, building a foundation for sustainable growth rather than chasing quick wins. By integrating strategic investment into your LLC's roadmap, you set the stage for enduring success and resilience in a competitive marketplace.

Evaluating Investment Opportunities Relevant to LLCs

When it comes to growing your LLC, making smart investment decisions is a crucial part of the strategy. Not every opportunity is built the same, and not every investment will align with the unique goals and structure of your LLC. Understanding how to evaluate these opportunities can save you from costly mistakes and ensure the money you allocate contributes meaningfully to your company's long-term success. This section covers how to critically assess investment options that suit your LLC's needs, financial health, and growth aspirations.

First and foremost, the evaluation process should start with clarity about your LLC's overarching goals. Are you aiming for rapid expansion, steady income generation, or perhaps diversification of revenue streams? Knowing what you want out of an investment helps filter the vast array of options out there. For instance, a startup LLC with limited capital might focus on investments that promise quicker returns or directly support core operations. On the other hand, a more established LLC may seek longer-term opportunities that build assets or rollout new products. This goal-setting framework creates a lens to view every investment through, making your decisions more disciplined and targeted.

Next, any investment decision needs a thorough examination of the financial implications. This goes beyond the surface-level expected returns or profit margins. You should analyze the capital required upfront, the timeline for return on investment (ROI), and the ongoing costs related to the opportunity. Some investments may seem attractive because of potentially high returns, but they could also come with bigger cash flow demands that might strain your LLC. Evaluating liquidity is key—meaning, how easily can your LLC recover its funds if the investment doesn't pan out? Always weigh if your current cash flow can sustain the new commitment without jeopardizing daily operations.

Another important factor is the risk profile of each potential investment. Every investment carries inherent risk, but understanding how that risk fits within your LLC's tolerance is vital. For LLC owners, risk consideration isn't just about potential loss of capital; it also involves examining how an investment might affect your business continuity and creditworthiness. Does the investment involve entering a new market you're unfamiliar with? Are there regulatory uncertainties linked to it? Do external economic factors play a heavy role here? Evaluating these risk components will help you avoid investments that might overextend your business or expose it to unmanaged vulnerabilities.

Additionally, assessing the alignment of an investment opportunity with your LLC's core competencies is crucial. It might be tempting to dive into trending sectors or lucrative deals, but if the venture falls outside the scope of your team's strengths, you may face operational challenges. For example, an LLC specializing in digital marketing might find it difficult to manage an investment in a physical retail location without the right expertise. Evaluating if the opportunity leverages your existing resources, knowledge, and network not only raises the likelihood of success but also minimizes missteps related to unfamiliar territory.

One cannot overlook the impact that market dynamics and timing have on investment evaluations. The best opportunities often depend on market conditions that favor your specific industry or geographic area. Conducting due diligence on current trends, consumer demand, competitor positioning, and even potential technological disruptions should be part of your evaluation toolkit. Also, timing your investment can be just as important as the nature of the investment. Jumping in too early or too late can significantly alter outcomes. Keep an eye on market cycles and shifts to make choices that optimize your LLC's competitive advantage.

Legal and regulatory considerations deserve your detailed attention as well. LLCs, depending on the state and industry, are subject to various laws that might impact an investment's feasibility. For example, real estate is a common investment avenue but comes with layers of zoning laws, property taxes, and environmental regulations that could complicate your LLC's involvement. Similarly, investing in new technologies might trigger intellectual property or licensing issues.

Consulting with legal advisors as part of your evaluation process will help you avoid surprises that could stall or derail your investment.

Evaluating how an investment fits into the bigger picture of your LLC's financial structure is also necessary. Some investments may require you to take on debt or dilute ownership if you're bringing in outside capital. Either of these outcomes changes your LLC's financial and operational landscape. You have to consider whether the potential returns justify these trade-offs. Being mindful of the impact on your company's balance sheet, capital reserves, and risk exposure will provide a clearer perspective on the true cost and benefit of an investment opportunity.

Don't overlook the importance of scalability when assessing investments. Growth-focused LLCs particularly benefit from opportunities that can expand in scope and profitability over time. For example, investing in proprietary software development might take longer to generate profit but could dramatically increase revenue streams as the business grows. Conversely, some investments might offer quicker returns but lack potential for future expansion. Balancing both types, or prioritizing scalability according to your LLC's growth trajectory, ensures that your investments contribute to sustainable growth rather than short-term gains alone.

Another practical way to evaluate investment opportunities is to leverage financial modeling tools. These allow you to simulate different scenarios and forecast how an investment could perform under varied conditions. Running projections on cash flow impact, ROI timelines, and even worst-case situations can deepen your understanding of the opportunity's risks and rewards. Such analysis helps remove emotional decision-making from the process, grounding choices in data and realistic expectations. Plus, well-prepared models can support discussions with financial advisors or potential partners.

It's also wise to consider the potential for diversification when selecting investments. A healthy portfolio helps spread risk and reduces dependence on a single revenue source. For many LLCs, especially those just getting started, concentrating investments too narrowly might seem safer but can leave the business vulnerable to market swings. Diversifying across different asset classes or industries can protect your LLC against economic changes and open up new channels for income. Still, smart diversification requires understanding each opportunity well enough to maintain a balanced and manageable investment portfolio.

Once you've done your homework, it's valuable to seek input from trusted advisors or industry peers. Entrepreneurs and LLC owners often benefit from the insights of others who've navigated similar investment decisions. Advisors can point out red flags you might have missed or highlight additional benefits worth considering. Peer feedback adds practical context to your analysis, especially if those peers operate in related industries or share similar organizational structures. This collaborative approach can strengthen your confidence in the final investment choice.

Finally, remember that evaluating investment opportunities is an ongoing process. Markets evolve, financial situations shift, and business goals adapt as your LLC grows. What seemed like a perfect investment six months ago might no longer fit your strategy or risk tolerance. Regularly revisit and reassess your investments to make tweaks or exit decisions as necessary. Keeping a dynamic perspective on your investments not only maximizes returns but also ensures your LLC remains agile in an ever-changing market environment.

In summary, evaluating investment opportunities for your LLC requires a careful balance of goal alignment, financial scrutiny, risk assessment, and adaptability. Taking the time upfront to analyze how an opportunity fits within your company's framework can prevent costly missteps and unlock valuable growth. Your LLC's success depends not just on finding opportunities, but on choosing the right ones and managing them effectively over time.

Balancing Risk and Return in LLC Investment Decisions

When it comes to growing your LLC through strategic investments, understanding how to balance risk and return is essential. Not every investment opportunity is created equal, and while the potential for high returns can be tempting, those rewards rarely come without a corresponding increase in risk. Striking the right balance means making choices that support sustainable growth while protecting your business from unnecessary setbacks. This isn't about avoiding risks altogether—that's impossible in business—but about managing those risks thoughtfully so they align with your firm's financial goals and capacity.

First, it's important to consider your LLC's unique circumstances—its financial health, business model, market position, and timeline for growth. An aggressive investment approach might work for a tech startup with venture capital backing and a long runway, but a local service-based LLC focused on steady cash flow may need a more conservative strategy. Recognizing where your LLC falls along this spectrum will help you set realistic expectations for returns and acceptable risk levels. Jumping headfirst into high-risk investments without this grounding can jeopardize everything you've built.

One of the key principles in balancing risk and return is diversification. Just as individuals diversify personal portfolios to avoid putting all their eggs in one basket, LLCs should consider spreading investments across different assets or opportunities. This might mean putting some capital in expanding product lines, some in marketing initiatives, or even in professional development or technology upgrades. Each avenue carries its own risk/return profile, and combined, they can create a more stable foundation for growth than focusing on a single "big win" investment.

Another factor to weigh carefully is the liquidity of your investments. Many small business owners make the mistake of investing heavily in illiquid assets, such as expensive equipment or long-term real estate, without maintaining enough operational flexibility. Those assets might appreciate or generate return over time, but they also tie up capital that could be needed for unexpected expenses or opportunities. Ensuring that part of your investment strategy keeps cash or near-cash reserves available provides a cushion that can be critical when facing market fluctuations or internal cash flow challenges.

Risk assessment isn't just about probabilities, it's about context. The same investment could have very different implications depending on your LLC's current financial stability. A risk that's manageable for a business consistently generating positive cash flow may be disastrous for one operating close to its break-even point. This underlines the necessity of regular financial review and realistic scenario planning. Looking at "what if" situations—like sudden sales drops or increased costs—helps anticipate how various risks impact your ability to weather the storm.

While risk is often framed negatively, it's important to understand that taking calculated risks is actually a driver of business growth. Without some risk, your LLC may stagnate. The challenge is in determining which risks are worth taking. Ideally, each investment decision should be tied to clearly defined business objectives: Are you trying to increase revenue quickly? Build long-term stability? Enter new markets? Knowing your goal helps prioritize investments that make sense for your growth story and risk tolerance.

To get more practical, consider developing a risk-return matrix tailored to your LLC. On one axis, place potential investments along a scale of risk—from low to high. On the other axis, rate expected returns similarly. This kind of visual tool can provide clarity when faced with multiple investment options, allowing you to compare and decide more systematically rather than emotionally. Investments that fall into the high-return, low-risk quadrant are ideal but rare; more often, you'll find a trade-off. Still, having this structure reduces guesswork and supports informed decision-making.

Additionally, don't overlook the importance of your LLC's overall capital structure when balancing risk and return. If your business is heavily leveraged—meaning it carries a significant amount of debt—the tolerance for risky investments should be low because the downside could be crippling. Conversely, if your LLC has built equity and operates with plenty of financial headroom, you might afford to pursue opportunities with more volatility. Understanding how your debt, equity, and cash reserves interplay shapes the baseline for safe yet opportunistic investing.

Another common pitfall is letting emotions or the fear of missing out drive investment choices. The excitement over a hot trend or the pressure from competitors can cloud judgment. Systematically evaluating investments through financial metrics such as internal rate of return (IRR), payback period, and net present value (NPV) keeps the decision grounded in data. These tools help you see beyond marketing promises and assess true profitability and risk adjusted for time and capital cost.

For many LLCs, partnering with financial advisors or business consultants can provide valuable perspective when weighing risk and return. Experts can spot potential red flags or growth areas that might not be obvious from inside the business, ensuring investment plans are robust and well thought out. At the same time, relying too heavily on outside opinions without internal analysis can be risky—ultimately, your business's risk appetite and strategy must come from your understanding of its unique situation.

Monitoring and adjusting your investment strategy over time is just as critical as making the initial decision. Markets change, new risks emerge, and your LLC's priorities evolve. What seemed like a balanced risk-return proposition last year might not look the same today. Establish regular check-ins to review how your investments are performing against expectations, and be prepared to pivot or divest when necessary. This dynamic management approach turns investment decisions from one-time impulses into part of a sustainable system that grows your LLC prudently.

Finally, don't forget to factor in non-financial risks that can affect your investment decisions—things like regulatory changes, industry disruptions, or shifts in customer preferences. While harder to quantify, these risks can have profound impacts on returns. Building a comprehensive risk framework that includes external environment scanning will help ensure your LLC's investments are resilient, not just lucrative at face value.

Balancing risk and return in LLC investment decisions is a nuanced but vital skill that drives effective strategic planning. It requires a clear-eyed understanding of your business's financial realities, a disciplined approach to diversification and liquidity, and continual review to adapt as conditions evolve. By managing risk thoughtfully, you empower your LLC to pursue growth opportunities with confidence, safeguarding your business's legacy and potential in an uncertain world.

Chapter 5: Protecting Your LLC Through Risk Mitigation

Running an LLC means facing uncertainties, so protecting your business with proactive risk mitigation is essential to long-term success. You'll want to identify potential financial threats early on and take deliberate steps to reduce exposure—whether from market shifts, operational hiccups, or legal complications. This involves more than just insurance; it includes creating policies that safeguard your assets, protecting your intellectual property, and maintaining clear contracts that minimize disputes. Taking action to reduce vulnerabilities not only shields your business from costly setbacks but also builds confidence with partners, lenders, and clients. Remember, risk mitigation is an ongoing process that evolves with your business—staying vigilant helps you turn challenges into opportunities instead of obstacles. Prioritize this to keep your LLC strong and resilient through every stage of growth.

Identifying Common Financial Risks Facing LLCs

Running an LLC means dealing with financial risks that could affect your business's stability and growth. Even if you have a solid business idea and a strong team, understanding the types of financial risks you face is essential. When you recognize these risks upfront, you can build strategies to avoid or minimize their impact. This section focuses specifically on the common financial risks confronting LLCs—not just the obvious pitfalls, but also the less apparent threats that can quietly erode your success.

One of the most straightforward risks is cash flow volatility. Many LLC owners assume that steady revenue means steady cash flow, but that's often not the case. Unpredictable expenses, seasonal sales patterns, or delayed customer payments can create painful cash shortages. These shortages might force you to delay paying bills, miss payroll deadlines, or turn down growth opportunities because you lack liquid funds. The challenge with cash flow risk is that even profitable businesses can fail if they can't maintain a consistent cash runway.

Closely related to cash flow is the problem of poor expense management. When you don't track or control your costs carefully, small overruns can snowball into major financial strain. LLCs often face this risk when they overcommit to fixed expenses like leases, utilities, or subscriptions without accounting for fluctuations in revenue. If your business expenses outpace income for too long, it can lead to debt accumulation or even insolvency.

Another typical financial risk for LLCs comes from relying too heavily on a limited number of clients. This concentration risk means that if a key customer leaves, your revenue could drop dramatically overnight. For example, losing even a single large contract or wholesale buyer can create a substantial financial hole. Diversifying your client base reduces this risk, but it's often easier said than done for small or new LLCs trying to gain traction.

Market risk also deserves attention, especially for LLCs operating in industries exposed to shifting consumer preferences, technological disruption, or economic cycles. Changes in demand, competitive pressures, or regulatory environments can cut into your margins or turnover without warning. For LLC owners, it's vital to monitor these external conditions regularly and anticipate how they might affect your revenue streams and cost structures.

Credit risk is another subtle but widespread hazard. This occurs when your business extends credit to customers who fail to pay on time—or worse, default entirely. Many LLCs, especially service providers and wholesalers, offer payment terms to encourage sales, but this can backfire if clients delay payments or dispute invoices. Maintaining healthy credit policies and performing due diligence before extending credit are key steps to avoid damaging your LLC's financial health.

Insurance-related financial risks can catch many LLC owners off guard. Without adequate coverage, a single liability claim, property loss, or business interruption event could lead to crippling out-of-pocket expenses. While some LLC owners understand the importance of insurance, they often underestimate the breadth of coverage needed or believe it's too costly. However, opting out or skimping on insurance can push your LLC into deep financial trouble after an unforeseen incident.

Legal risks represent another crucial financial threat. LLCs provide a protective shield for personal assets, but they're not invincible. Lawsuits, contract disputes, or compliance failures can incur hefty legal fees, settlements, and regulatory penalties. Even if your LLC isn't at fault, defending against legal actions can drain resources and distract your focus from growing the business. Understanding the legal landscape and working closely with professionals to draft airtight contracts and maintain regulatory compliance helps buffer this risk.

Interest rate risk might seem tailored for large corporations or financial institutions, but it matters for LLCs financing their operations or expansion through loans and credit lines. If your debt carries a variable interest rate, rising rates can significantly increase your repayment amounts, squeezing profit margins and cash flow. This risk is especially relevant when the economy is volatile or the Federal

Reserve signals potential rate hikes. Structuring your financing thoughtfully can reduce exposure to sudden interest rate shifts.

Economic downturns and recessions form a broad but very real financial risk for almost every LLC. During tougher economic times, consumers and businesses may cut back on spending, which reduces demand for your products or services. Access to credit can also tighten, further constraining cash flow. Even though you can't control macroeconomic forces, preparing for them by maintaining cash reserves and flexible cost structures can help your LLC weather these storms more effectively.

Fraud and financial mismanagement present yet another significant risk. Small LLCs sometimes face internal threats like employee theft, embezzlement, or inaccurate bookkeeping. The absence of strong internal controls and transparent financial oversight leaves the door open for these costly mistakes. Establishing clear financial policies, regular audits, and accountability within your LLC can guard against this risk.

Another form of risk that often gets overlooked is technological risk. Many LLCs rely on digital payment systems, accounting software, and online banking. A cyberattack, data breach, or system failure could result in financial losses through fraud, theft, or operational downtime. As technology integrates deeper into business operations, protecting your LLC from IT-related financial risks becomes a critical priority. Consider cybersecurity solutions and data backup plans as part of your risk mitigation strategy.

Finally, there's the risk associated with inadequate financial planning and forecasting. LLCs that fail to plan ahead often take unnecessary financial gambles or miss warning signs of trouble until it's too late. Without regular forecasting, it's difficult to spot coming shortfalls, plan resource allocation wisely, or pivot your strategy when the market shifts. Adopting proactive financial management tools and maintaining discipline in monitoring your LLC's financial health reduce this risk substantially.

Identifying these risks is the first step toward building a resilient LLC. While not every risk will apply equally to all businesses, most LLC owners will encounter several of these challenges at some point. The key is staying vigilant and addressing each potential threat before it becomes a crisis. Developing a culture of risk awareness within your LLC empowers you to take control of your financial future rather than reacting defensively to problems after they arise.

Every decision you make around spending, investing, insuring, and financing your LLC has some degree of risk attached. Understanding which risks are most likely to impact your unique business helps you prioritize actions that safeguard your assets and create a foundation for sustained growth. In the next section, we'll explore specific tools and strategies to shield your LLC from these financial risks through legal protections and insurance programs, but for now, recognizing these common dangers sets the groundwork for effective risk mitigation.

Implementing Insurance and Legal Safeguards for LLCs

When running an LLC, protecting your business from unexpected setbacks is crucial. One of the most effective ways to shield your company's financial well-being is by implementing the right insurance coverage alongside robust legal safeguards. These measures work hand in hand to reduce liability, protect assets, and ensure your LLC remains on solid footing no matter what challenges arise. Without this protective layer, even a single lawsuit or unforeseen event can cripple your operation financially and damage your reputation.

Insurance coverage tailored for LLCs is not just a smart choice; it's an essential one. Several types of insurance can fill specific risk gaps that LLCs commonly face. General liability insurance, for instance, covers claims related to bodily injury, property damage, or advertising mistakes. This kind of coverage is often the first line of defense, safeguarding your business against costly litigation or settlements resulting from accidents or negligence. Since LLCs frequently engage with the public and vendors, this protection is almost always necessary.

Beyond general liability, entrepreneurs should consider professional liability insurance, sometimes called errors and omissions insurance, especially if the LLC provides services or professional advice. Mistakes or oversights in service delivery can lead to claims that can drain your financial resources. Having this insurance gives you confidence in offering your services without fearing that a single error will bring financial ruin.

Property insurance is another important consideration. If your LLC owns or rents physical space, equipment, or inventory, having insurance that covers damage from fire, theft, or natural disasters can mean the difference between a swift recovery and permanent closure. Many small business owners underestimate the scope and frequency of such incidents, so securing property insurance tailored to your business's size and needs is a proactive move.

For LLCs with employees, workers' compensation insurance often comes into play. It's typically required by law and protects employees who are injured on the job by covering medical costs and lost wages. Not only does this safeguard your team, but it also shields your LLC from potentially expensive lawsuits related to workplace injuries. Prioritizing this coverage can build trust with employees and demonstrate your commitment to their well-being, boosting overall morale and loyalty.

While insurance effectively manages external risks, legal safeguards address internal vulnerabilities and your LLC's structural integrity. The single most important legal protection is maintaining the LLC's separate legal status. This means adhering strictly to corporate formalities: keeping business and personal finances separate, properly documenting all transactions, and ensuring compliance with state filing requirements. If you blur these lines, courts may pierce the corporate veil, exposing your personal assets to business liabilities.

Another critical legal safeguard involves drafting comprehensive operating agreements. Even if your state does not require one, an operating agreement is invaluable because it clearly defines roles, responsibilities, and decision-making processes among members. This reduces the likelihood of internal disputes and provides a concrete reference if disagreements escalate. Properly crafted agreements can also include provisions on how to handle liabilities, member buyouts, and dissolution, saving headaches and legal expenses down the road.

Utilizing legal documents like contracts and waivers is another fundamental step. Well-written contracts with vendors, clients, and employees clarify expectations and responsibilities, reducing ambiguity that often triggers litigation. Including indemnity clauses and limitation of liability provisions further protects your LLC from excessive exposure in disputes. Remember, the absence of solid contracts invites unnecessary risk.

Complying with licensing, permits, and regulatory requirements specific to your industry or location also plays a key role. Ignoring or overlooking regulations can lead to fines, penalties, or forced shutdowns. Keeping your LLC in good legal standing not only protects its operations but also enhances its credibility when negotiating partnerships or securing financing.

Employing risk mitigation doesn't stop with setting up insurance and legal frameworks; it requires ongoing attention. Regularly reviewing your insurance policies to ensure adequate and current coverage is vital as your LLC grows and changes. For example, expanding your product line or hiring additional staff will likely necessitate adjusting coverage limits or adding new policies. Similarly, periodic legal checkups help identify weaknesses in contracts or operating agreements, allowing prompt updates that align with your evolving business needs.

It's important to consult experienced professionals when implementing these protections. Licensed insurance agents specializing in small businesses can help identify the right combination of policies, balancing cost against coverage. Likewise, an attorney familiar with LLC law can draft or review your operating agreement and contracts to make sure they're airtight and customized to your business model. While these experts come at a cost, the investment often saves far more by preventing costly pitfalls.

Additionally, considering umbrella insurance policies can provide an extra layer of security beyond standard coverage limits. This type of policy activates when your basic liability insurance caps are reached, offering broader protection against large claims or lawsuits. For growing LLCs whose risks become increasingly complex, umbrella insurance adds peace of mind, ensuring that a single catastrophic event won't lead to financial devastation.

Although it might feel tempting to skip some safeguards, especially when funds are tight, the financial consequences of going unprotected far outweigh the upfront expenses. Lawsuits can arise unexpectedly, and without the proper insurance or legal defenses in place, your LLC could lose not only money but also valuable time and reputation. Taking action to limit risk demonstrates responsible management and helps attract investors, lenders, and clients who favor businesses that handle their risks proactively.

Lastly, don't underestimate the value of establishing good communication channels within your LLC when it comes to risk management. Keep all members informed about insurance updates, legal changes, and compliance requirements. Encourage a culture where team members feel responsible for recognizing and reporting potential risks early. When everyone understands the stakes, you create a united front that's better prepared to handle challenges swiftly and efficiently.

Implementing insurance and legal safeguards for your LLC is not a one-time event but an ongoing commitment. It's about continuously protecting your business's financial health while creating a stable foundation for growth. By thoughtfully selecting coverage options and establishing clear legal boundaries, your LLC will be well-positioned to survive and thrive amid uncertainties. This proactive approach reflects the hallmark of a savvy entrepreneur who values both opportunity and protection.

Chapter 6: Financing Options Tailored for LLCs

When it comes to funding your LLC, understanding the range of options available can make all the difference in finding the right fit for your business needs and growth stage. Traditional bank loans often offer competitive rates but come with stringent requirements that may be challenging for new or smaller LLCs, while alternative sources like online lenders, crowdfunding, and venture capital provide more flexible solutions that can be tapped depending on your industry and credit profile. Each approach carries distinct pros and cons, so it's crucial to align your financing strategy with your LLC's unique financial health, goals, and risk tolerance. By carefully evaluating these options upfront, you can secure the capital necessary to fuel operations, invest in opportunities, and ultimately steer your LLC toward sustainable success.

Comparing Traditional and Alternative Funding for LLCs

When it comes to financing your LLC, understanding the differences between traditional and alternative funding sources is essential. Each type has its advantages, limitations, and ideal use cases. Choosing the right option can influence your business's financial health and growth trajectory. Traditional funding methods, such as bank loans and credit lines, have been the backbone of business financing for decades. Alternative funding options, on the other hand, have emerged more recently to fill gaps that traditional lenders often overlook, making them vital tools for many LLC owners.

Traditional funding typically involves borrowing money from banks, credit unions, or established financial institutions. These lenders offer structured loan programs with set terms, fixed or variable interest rates, and repayment schedules. The appeal lies in their predictability and usually lower cost of capital compared to many alternative options. Banks often require solid credit histories, detailed financial documentation, and collateral to secure loans for LLCs. This setup benefits stable companies with reliable cash flow and good credit profiles. However, it can pose significant hurdles for newer LLCs or those operating in industries perceived as riskier.

Alternative funding sources, including peer-to-peer lending, online lenders, invoice factoring, and crowdfunding, offer more flexibility but usually at a higher cost. These options cater to LLCs that might struggle to meet the rigid criteria of traditional lenders. For instance, many online lenders approve funds faster and require less documentation. Invoice factoring allows businesses to use outstanding invoices to access quick cash, which is particularly helpful for companies with delayed customer payments. Crowdfunding enables your LLC to raise capital from multiple investors, often without giving up equity or incurring traditional debt. These alternatives add versatility but need to be approached with care due to their varied fee structures and potential impacts on your LLC's financial stability.

The approval process differs significantly between traditional and alternative lenders. Banks typically demand thorough credit checks, business plans, and several months or years of detailed financial records. LLCs with limited operational histories or inconsistent revenue streams often find it challenging to qualify. In contrast, many alternative lenders rely more heavily on cash flow projections, business model viability, or even social proof from crowdfunding campaigns. This faster approval boosts agility, allowing LLCs to capitalize on timely opportunities or manage emergencies. Yet, faster approval can sometimes mean higher interest rates or fees, making it critical to balance speed with affordability.

Interest rates and repayment terms also paint contrasting pictures between these two funding categories. Traditional loans normally feature competitive interest rates, reflecting the lower risk banks perceive when dealing with well-established LLCs. Terms often extend over several years, offering manageable monthly payments. This can help with long-term planning and preserving cash flow. Alternative lenders sometimes charge steeper rates or require repayment over shorter durations, as seen with merchant cash advances or short-term online loans. This increased cost catches many LLC owners off guard, so understanding the full implications of each funding option's pricing structure is key before making a commitment.

Both traditional and alternative funding influence your LLC's credit profile in different ways. Successfully repaying a bank loan builds a solid credit history, potentially unlocking larger funding pools in the future. Traditional debt tends to be reported to major credit bureaus, impacting your LLC's credit score positively when managed well. Meanwhile, several alternative lenders might only report some or none of their financed loans, which means your repayment habits might not enhance your creditworthiness directly. However, failing to meet obligations on alternative funding can still damage your reputation and access to future resources.

Another important factor is the potential impact on control and ownership of your LLC. Most traditional loans don't require giving up equity or business control; they're purely debt-based. Meanwhile, some alternative funding avenues like equity crowdfunding or private investors involve selling a piece of your LLC in exchange for capital. This may dilute your ownership and decision-making power, which isn't always ideal for owners wanting to maintain tight control. That said, if your LLC is in an early stage or growth phase, tapping equity-based alternatives might be a strategic way to access funds without debt burdens.

Accessibility plays a major role in deciding between traditional and alternative funding. Established banks can be difficult for newly formed or niche LLCs to penetrate due to their conservative lending standards. Startups or businesses in emerging industries may have limited credit history and financial data to present, reducing their eligibility. In contrast, alternative lenders often focus more on the business's potential and current cash flow rather than extensive paperwork, making financing more attainable. This can be a lifesaver for LLCs in dynamic markets or those looking for quick capital injections. However, the trade-off often comes in higher costs, requiring thoughtful evaluation.

From a strategic perspective, blending traditional and alternative funding can serve an LLC's unique needs effectively. For example, a stable LLC might use a traditional bank loan for long-term investments like equipment or real estate, benefiting from lower interest rates. Simultaneously, it could rely on alternative financing such as short-term loans or invoice factoring to manage cyclical cash flow gaps or sudden expenses. This diversified approach minimizes risk and keeps cash flow manageable, ensuring the business can weather financial ebbs and flows without becoming over-leveraged in one funding form.

It's also worth recognizing the evolving landscape of financing. Advances in technology and financial innovation continue to expand access to alternative funding options. Digital platforms make loan applications and approvals faster and more transparent, while crowdfunding and peer-to-peer lending democratize access to capital. LLC owners equipped with this knowledge can shop around, compare offers, and tailor their financing strategies with more precision than ever before.

Despite the potential benefits of alternative funding, it's crucial to scrutinize all terms carefully. The urgency or ease of access might tempt LLC owners to commit to unfavorable agreements, such as hidden fees or balloon payments. Legal advice or consulting with a financial advisor can help ensure the chosen funding aligns with your LLC's goals and cash flow capabilities. Overextending your business with high-cost debt or giving up too much control can stunt growth rather than fuel it.

Creditworthiness remains a key driver of which funding path you can pursue. Consistent revenue, solid financial records, and good personal or business credit scores will always improve your chances of securing affordable traditional loans. If your LLC currently lacks these, consider focusing on strengthening them before seeking large-scale funding. Leveraging alternative funding might fill in the gaps during this period, but treat it as a stepping stone rather than a permanent solution.

Ultimately, comparing traditional and alternative funding for LLCs comes down to understanding your business's current financial standing, growth plans, and risk tolerance. Traditional options provide predictable, cost-effective capital if you can qualify, while alternative solutions offer flexibility and speed at a premium. By assessing these trade-offs honestly and aligning your funding with your LLC's unique circumstances, you position your business to thrive financially and take advantage of opportunities as they arise.

Preparing Effective Loan Applications and Investor Pitches for LLCs

Securing financing stands as one of the most critical steps toward driving your LLC forward. Whether you're aiming for a traditional bank loan or courting private investors, how you present your business can make or break your chances. The journey begins with crafting loan applications and investor pitches that communicate not only your LLC's financial viability but also your vision and commitment. This section focuses on practical ways to prepare documents and presentations that resonate, inspire confidence, and increase your likelihood of success.

Before putting pen to paper, it's essential to understand that lenders and investors aren't just looking for numbers. They want to see a comprehensive story demonstrating your LLC's potential. A loan officer or investor expects more than financial data—they want insight into how your business operates, what differentiates it, and how you plan to use the funds responsibly. This means every application or pitch needs to balance clear, concise facts with a compelling narrative about your LLC's unique value and trajectory.

Start with your LLC's core financial documents. A well-prepared loan application or pitch hinges on credible and thorough financial statements like your balance sheet, income statement, and cash flow projections. These provide a snapshot of your LLC's current health and future prospects. Pay close attention to accuracy and clarity; errors or inconsistencies in your charts and numbers can quickly erode trust. It's best to have these reviewed by a financial advisor or accountant to reinforce credibility.

When drafting your loan application, clarity is king. Most loan officers skim applications quickly, so your ability to organize information logically will set you apart. Break the application down into sections: company overview, ownership and management structure, purpose of the loan, detailed use of funds, and financial statements. Each segment should be direct and free of jargon, making it easy for reviewers to grasp your LLC's story and needs without wading through complexity.

Investor pitches, while sharing some similarities with loan applications, tend to require more storytelling to spark interest and emotional engagement. Investors want to understand your LLC's market opportunity and competitive edge. Begin your pitch by outlining the problem your business solves and who your target market is. Then, clearly explain your product or service, what sets it apart, and how your LLC plans to capture market share. This section should highlight market research and tangible proof of demand where possible.

Investors expect transparency about your LLC's risks as well. Addressing potential challenges candidly signals you've done your homework and aren't blindly optimistic. Present strategies you've devised to mitigate these risks. Whether it's competition, regulatory issues, or operational hurdles, showing awareness and preparedness builds confidence. Avoid painting an unrealistically rosy picture.

Another crucial ingredient in investor pitches is the explanation of your LLC's revenue model. How will you make money? Outline your pricing strategy, sales channels, and any partnerships or contracts that lend credibility to future income projections. Investors appreciate seeing both short-term wins and longer-term sustainability in your plan. Incorporating milestones or traction metrics—such as customer acquisition rates, product launch dates, or revenue benchmarks—illustrates momentum and a clear path forward.

Loan officers, too, prioritize understanding how you intend to repay borrowed funds. Demonstrating a realistic repayment strategy reassures lenders that their money is secure. This involves presenting cash flow forecasts that align with your requested loan amount and repayment terms. Make sure your projections are conservative and backed by logical assumptions based on industry standards and your LLC's actual performance.

One often-overlooked element in both loan and investor documentation is your LLC's management team. The people steering the ship matter greatly to funders. Brief biographies emphasizing the experience, skills, and past successes of key members can add a layer of trustworthiness. Investors invest in people as much as ideas, so showcasing your team's capacity to execute plans can tip the balance in your favor.

Visual presentation matters too. Whether written or oral, your application and pitch must be polished and professional. Use graphs and charts judiciously to support the narrative without overwhelming the audience with data. Formatting should be clean—consider bullet points for lists, bold headings for clarity, and concise paragraphs for easy reading. If you're delivering your pitch in person or via video, practice your delivery to maintain a confident and engaging presence. Rehearsing with trusted colleagues who can provide constructive feedback helps refine your approach.

To build credibility, supporting documents such as business licenses, contracts, or letters of recommendation can bolster your case. These extras don't just pad the packet; they provide tangible proof backing your claims. For example, a letter from a satisfied supplier or client can reinforce your LLC's reliability. Likewise, including credit history reports or personal financial statements when required signals transparency.

Timing and customization play roles that shouldn't be underestimated. One-size-fits-all applications rarely succeed. Tailor your loan applications and investor pitches to the specific funder's criteria and preferences. Research their priorities—some lenders might focus intensely on cash flow, while certain investors emphasize innovation or scalability. Align your materials to highlight the elements that resonate most with your audience's objectives.

It's important to build relationships early, too. Establishing contact with lenders or investors before submitting formal applications can open doors. This allows you to gather insights into what they're looking for, receive informal feedback, and adjust your materials accordingly. A casual conversation or introductory meeting can also personalize your request, shifting it from just another document to a real story with a real entrepreneur.

Remember, rejection is often part of the journey. If the first pitch or application doesn't succeed, seek feedback and refine your approach. Each submission should hone your messaging, fix gaps, and sharpen your financials. Persistence combined with learning transforms setbacks into stepping stones. Successful LLC owners treat every attempt as an opportunity to get stronger rather than as a failure.

When your documents and pitch align with clear financial data, authentic storytelling, and polished presentation, you build trust and confidence with potential funders. This foundation gives your LLC the best shot at securing funding that fuels growth. Focus on honesty, preparation, and alignment with funder expectations to move your financing efforts from hope to reality.

Chapter 7: Managing LLC Financial Records and Reporting

Keeping precise and organized financial records is the cornerstone of any successful LLC, as it not only ensures compliance with legal requirements but also empowers you to make informed business decisions with confidence. A disciplined approach to documenting every transaction, expense, and income stream lays the groundwork for accurate financial reporting, which in turn provides clarity on your LLC's financial health. By establishing consistent record-keeping routines and leveraging these reports, you can identify trends, spot inefficiencies, and prepare for upcoming financial obligations before they become problems. Ultimately, managing your LLC's financial records with care isn't just an administrative chore—it's a powerful tool that fuels growth, enables strategic planning, and builds trust with investors, lenders, and partners alike.

Best Practices for Maintaining Accurate LLC Financial Records

Accurate financial records form the backbone of a successful LLC. Without reliable records, decision-making becomes guesswork, taxes become a minefield, and growth opportunities are harder to spot and seize. Keeping your financial data precise and up-to-date isn't just about compliance—it's about empowering your business to thrive.

Every entrepreneur managing an LLC should adopt best practices that make record-keeping efficient, consistent, and legally sound.

Start by establishing a routine. Daily or weekly tracking of income and expenses ensures that nothing slips through the cracks. When you let receipts pile up or transactions go unrecorded for weeks, you're inviting errors and stress. Creating a schedule for bookkeeping tasks—whether that's reconciling bank statements every Sunday evening or logging every expense immediately after it occurs—makes accuracy a habit. Over time, this routine reduces stress when tax season rolls around and equips you to answer important financial questions quickly.

Organization is another cornerstone of financial accuracy. Use clearly labeled folders—either physical or digital—to separate categories like invoices, bills, bank statements, and payroll records. Don't wait until the end of the quarter to sort your paperwork; organize transactions and documentation as they come. If you're using software tools, take advantage of features like tagging or categorizing expenses by project or department. This not only simplifies monthly reviews but also makes it easier to spot anomalies or unusual trends before they grow into bigger issues.

Choosing the right bookkeeping system plays a critical role. Whether it's a simple spreadsheet for very small LLCs or cloud-based accounting software, select the tool that matches your business's complexity and your comfort with financial management. Off-the-shelf solutions like QuickBooks, Xero, or FreshBooks offer automation and integration with your bank accounts, cutting down manual errors. Plus, many have mobile apps that let you capture receipts on the go. However, no software can replace careful attention to detail and consistent data entry routines. It pays to understand the basics of double-entry bookkeeping so you can spot mistakes early on.

Separating business and personal finances is non-negotiable for LLC owners. Mixing the two is a common pitfall that complicates your accounting and can jeopardize your liability protection. Open a dedicated business bank account and credit card, and insist on running all LLC-related transactions through them. This clarity simplifies tax filings, audits, and financial analysis. Plus, lenders and investors appreciate seeing clean, well-maintained financial records tied directly to your business activities.

Keep an eye on vendor and client payments as part of maintaining accurate records. Track your accounts payable and accounts receivable diligently to avoid late fees and to maintain good credit standing. Implementing invoicing systems that send automatic reminders for overdue payments can help manage cash flow and improve your LLC's financial health. On the vendor side, paying bills on time preserves supplier relationships and lets you take advantage of early payment discounts where available.

Backing up your financial data is often overlooked but absolutely essential. Whether your records live on a computer, external hard drive, or cloud service, ensure multiple copies exist in separate locations. Data loss from hardware failure, theft, or cyberattacks can cripple your business. Regular backups combined with strong password protection guard against these risks and guarantee continuity in your record-keeping efforts.

Another best practice is reconciling your accounts regularly—monthly, at minimum. This process involves comparing your internal financial records with bank and credit card statements to identify discrepancies. Reconciliation helps catch fraud, recording errors, or misunderstandings about payments. When discrepancies arise, investigate them immediately rather than deferring correction. Staying on top of reconciliations keeps your financial picture accurate and trustworthy, building confidence whether you're talking to lenders, partners, or tax authorities.

Documenting your financial policies and procedures benefits everyone involved in managing your LLC's money. Clear guidelines on expense approvals, reimbursement processes, and data entry standards remove ambiguity. If your LLC has multiple members or employees, agreeing on these standards upfront avoids costly misunderstandings. Well-documented processes also support smoother transitions if you bring on new financial staff or outsource bookkeeping to a professional.

Staying compliant with legal requirements is fundamental. LLCs face various rules depending on their state and the nature of their business. Maintaining accurate financial records not only provides a trail for tax reporting but also satisfies regulatory audits. Keep all supporting documents—receipts, contracts, payroll records—for the duration required by tax authorities (usually 3 to 7 years). This systematic approach shields your LLC from penalties and legal headaches down the road.

Building a relationship with a qualified accountant or bookkeeping professional can elevate how your LLC handles financial records. Even if you manage day-to-day bookkeeping yourself, a professional review can provide invaluable insights and catch issues you might miss. Accountants also keep you informed about changing tax laws and help prepare financial statements that reflect a true and fair view of your business's health. Consider scheduling quarterly or biannual consultations to keep your LLC's finances in top shape.

Transparency with your fellow LLC members is another best practice to maintain trust and clear financial communication. Regular financial reporting keeps everyone aligned on the business's performance and obligations. Share profit and loss summaries, balance sheets, and cash flow statements during member meetings. Open dialogue around finances fosters accountability and can highlight areas needing attention before they escalate.

Integrating digital tools that support automation saves time and reduces human error, but don't rely solely on technology. Always cross-check automated entries for accuracy and completeness. Automation is a powerful supplement to rigorous bookkeeping practices, not a replacement. Furthermore, ensure that software access is limited to trusted individuals and that you regularly update security settings to protect sensitive financial data.

Maintain a mindset of continuous improvement when it comes to financial record-keeping. As your LLC grows or its business model evolves, periodically revisit your bookkeeping methods to accommodate new challenges or opportunities. Staying flexible and open to upgrading tools and processes can make the difference between merely surviving and thriving financially.

Lastly, view accurate record-keeping as an investment—not just a chore. Clear, well-maintained financial records equip you to make smarter decisions, secure better financing terms, and strategically plan your LLC's future. They reduce uncertainty and empower you to focus on growth, innovation, and competition in your market. Developing discipline around these best practices today lays the groundwork for your LLC's lasting financial success and operational resilience.

Utilizing Financial Reports to Drive LLC Business Decisions

Financial reports are more than just numbers on a page; they are vital tools that guide the direction and growth of your LLC. When you learn to interpret these documents effectively, you transform raw data into actionable insights that can shape your business strategy. Whether your LLC is just starting out or already established, leveraging financial reports helps you make informed decisions rather than relying on guesswork or assumptions.

At the core of any LLC's financial reporting are statements like the balance sheet, income statement, and cash flow statement. Each one offers a unique perspective on the health and performance of your business. The balance sheet reveals your company's net worth at a particular moment, showing assets, liabilities, and equity. The income statement provides a snapshot of profitability over a chosen timeframe by detailing revenues and expenses. Meanwhile, the cash flow statement tracks the movement of cash in and out, which is critical for maintaining day-to-day operations. Using these reports collectively gives you a comprehensive understanding of your business's financial status.

But understanding these reports is just the starting point. The real value emerges when you dig into the details and start asking tough questions. Are sales revenue growing consistently? What trends are visible in your expenses? How much cash is available versus what's tied up in accounts receivable or inventory? When these questions become part of your regular review, your financial reports turn into strategic tools that highlight opportunities and warn of potential pitfalls.

Consider, for instance, an LLC facing tight profit margins. By analyzing the income statement closely, you may spot rising costs that are eating into profits. This could be anything from increasing supplier prices to operational inefficiencies. Identifying this early enables timely action—whether negotiating better supplier contracts, streamlining processes, or adjusting pricing strategies. Without that careful review, these issues can go unnoticed until they threaten the viability of the business.

Financial reports also empower you to evaluate performance against your goals. If you've set clear targets for revenue growth or expense reduction, comparing them with actual figures highlights where your LLC is on track or falling short. This alignment between planning and reporting keeps your business accountable. It encourages regular check-ins and data-driven adjustments—key habits for long-term success and sustainability.

Moreover, these reports can guide decisions about resource allocation. As an entrepreneur, you have finite resources like time, capital, and personnel. Financial reports clarify which parts of your business generate the strongest returns and which consume more resources than they contribute. This insight helps prioritize investments in product development, marketing, or new hires. Instead of spreading resources thin, you focus them where they'll make the most impact.

Another critical aspect where financial reports make a difference is cash management. LLC owners often find themselves challenged by cash flow gaps, especially when seasonal patterns or client payment delays come into play. The cash flow statement provides early warning signs by mapping actual cash inflows and outflows. When you spot consistent shortfalls, you can explore solutions such as adjusting payment terms, securing short-term financing, or controlling discretionary spending. Proactive cash flow management prevents crises and keeps your operations running smoothly.

It's also worth noting that financial reports are indispensable when dealing with lenders, investors, or partners. Whether you're seeking a loan, attracting new investors, or collaborating with members, clear and up-to-date reporting builds trust and credibility. These stakeholders want evidence that your LLC is financially sound and capable of delivering returns. Transparent, well-prepared reports convey professionalism and increase your chances of securing favorable terms and support.

Data from financial reports can also fuel strategic planning initiatives. For example, analyzing revenue by product line or service can reveal which offerings your customers value most, and where there might be room for expansion or improvement. You can identify underperforming products or markets and decide if they deserve more resources or should be phased out. Integrating this kind of financial analysis with market research results creates a robust foundation for smart growth strategies.

In addition, regular examination of financial ratios derived from these reports adds another layer of insight. Ratios like current ratio, debt-to-equity, gross profit margin, and return on investment are shorthand gauges of your business's financial health. Monitoring these over time helps you spot trends such as increasing debt levels or shrinking profit margins before they become critical. Your ability to act early can mean the difference between righting the ship and scrambling to recover from financial strain.

For LLC owners juggling multiple roles, financial reports serve as a reality check. It's easy to get caught up in daily operational demands and lose sight of overall financial performance. Setting a recurring schedule to review your reports—monthly or quarterly—creates discipline and ensures you stay connected to your company's financial pulse. These sessions become the forum for honest evaluation and strategic conversations instead of reactive firefighting.

Technology also plays a significant role here. Using accounting software that generates real-time financial reports makes it simpler to access and interpret your data. Many tools provide customizable dashboards and visualizations, allowing you to spot key trends at a glance without wading through piles of spreadsheets. Leveraging these digital aids lets you focus more on analysis and action rather than data entry and number crunching.

Ultimately, consistent use of financial reports molds an entrepreneurial mindset grounded in facts and evidence. It trains you to see beyond just profit or loss, prompting a deeper understanding of how cash flow, costs, assets, and liabilities interconnect. This knowledge transforms managing your LLC from a reactive task to strategic stewardship. It equips you weather challenges and capitalize on opportunities with confidence and clarity.

In practice, many successful LLC owners combine their financial reports with other business insights, such as customer feedback and industry benchmarks, to create a holistic view. Financial reports tell you what's happening; other data helps explain why it's happening. Together, they become a powerful decision-making toolkit. Lean into your financial statements—they're more than bookkeeping artifacts. When used wisely, they generate the insight you need to steer your LLC onto a profitable, sustainable path.

To sum up, financial reports aren't simply end-of-period chores or regulatory obligations—they're active instruments for growth, control, and clarity. By immersing yourself in these reports, you build a solid foundation to make smarter decisions that enhance profitability, improve cash flow, and strengthen resilience. Just as a captain navigates a ship by reading the stars and gauges, your role as an LLC owner depends on reading and acting on your financial reports with precision and purpose.

Chapter 8: Understanding LLC Profit Distribution Strategies

When it comes to distributing profits in an LLC, having a solid strategy is crucial for maintaining harmony among members and ensuring the business stays financially healthy. Unlike traditional corporations, LLCs offer flexibility in how profits are allocated, which means you can tailor distributions to match each member's contribution, role, or agreement—provided that you've clearly outlined these terms in your operating agreement. Profit distribution isn't just about divvying up money; it's about aligning incentives, managing cash flow, and planning for reinvestment or growth opportunities. Awareness of how different distribution methods affect tax obligations also plays a vital role in choosing the right approach. By understanding and applying clear profit distribution strategies early on, LLC owners can avoid confusion, minimize disputes, and create a financial environment that supports both individual and business success.

Methods for Allocating Profits Among LLC Members

When you're running an LLC, deciding how to allocate profits among members is one of the most critical financial decisions you'll face. Unlike corporations, where dividends are typically distributed based on stock ownership, LLCs offer a lot more flexibility. This flexibility can be a major advantage, but it can also introduce complexity if the profit-sharing method isn't clearly defined from the start. Profit allocation affects not only how members get compensated but also how taxes are handled and how future business decisions are made.

One of the most common ways LLCs allocate profits is through **ownership percentage**. This approach is straightforward: profits are divided in proportion to each member's capital contribution or agreed ownership interest. For example, if one member owns 60% of the LLC and another owns 40%, profits might be split 60/40 accordingly. This method is often seen as fair and easy to administer, especially for LLCs where members contribute capital upfront and expect returns relative to their stake. It minimizes disputes because allocations reflect each person's initial and ongoing investment in the company.

However, pure ownership percentage-based allocation doesn't always match the reality of members' involvement or value contribution. Some members might invest more time, expertise, or take on more operational risk, while others may be passive investors. That mismatch can lead to tension if profits don't reflect those efforts. Fortunately, LLCs can customize profit distribution using **special allocations**, which allow members to receive profits disproportionate to ownership stakes. This flexibility enables an LLC to reward active participants or incentivize key contributors differently.

Special allocations commonly show up in LLC agreements as profit splits based on roles or responsibilities rather than capital contribution alone. For instance, a managing member who runs day-to-day operations may receive a guaranteed percentage of profits or a priority return before residual profits are divided among others. Similarly, members who provide critical expertise or intellectual property might negotiate higher allocations to compensate for their added value. These methods motivate members to engage deeply with the business and can support growth by acknowledging contributions beyond money.

Another important method is the use of **preferred returns**. This approach grants certain members a fixed return on their investment before any remaining profits are distributed. Preferred returns act somewhat like interest payments, providing a degree of financial security to investors who may want to minimize risk exposure. Once the preferred return is paid, profits can then be split among members based on another agreed method, like ownership percentage. Preferred returns work well for LLCs seeking outside investors who prioritize steady gains over direct control.

Allocating profits on a **guaranteed payments** basis is also common, especially for members performing services actively. Guaranteed payments function like salaries paid to members regardless of LLC profitability. This means the member is compensated for services before profits are allocated. The remaining profit pool can then be divided according to ownership percentages or any other agreed-upon formula. Guaranteed payments clarify compensation for work rendered and ensure active members are rewarded fairly, reducing disputes related to workload versus financial return.

Beyond these approaches, some LLCs use **sweep accounts** or **reinvestment plans** as part of their profit allocation strategy. In these cases, a portion of profits might be held back within the LLC to fund growth initiatives, pay down debt, or build reserves instead of being immediately distributed. The remaining profits are shared among members according to the agreed split. This method supports long-term financial health by balancing member payouts with business needs. For entrepreneurs planning aggressive growth or cyclical industries, retaining earnings is often critical for stability and opportunity.

Allocating profits can also involve hybrid strategies combining several methods to reflect the unique makeup and goals of the LLC. For example, an LLC could provide guaranteed payments to operational members, pay preferred returns to investing members, and divide the residual profits proportionally. Structuring profit allocations to align incentives with contributions and expectations ensures fairness and keeps members motivated. Such tailored arrangements should always be meticulously documented in the operating agreement to avoid confusion or legal challenges later on.

While flexibility is valuable, it's essential to establish **clear, written agreements** about profit distribution before launching the LLC. Verbal promises or informal understandings often lead to disputes that drain resources and morale. Members should work together to draft a detailed operating agreement that outlines exactly how profits will be shared, including conditions for distributions, timing, and methods for handling losses. These documents can also include processes for revisiting and adjusting profit allocation as the business evolves, keeping the strategy aligned with changing circumstances.

Another practical consideration is the need for profit allocations to comply with tax rules. Although detailed tax analysis falls outside this section's scope, it's worth noting that profit allocation methods can have significant tax consequences for members. Generally, LLC profit and loss distributions pass through to members' individual returns, reflecting their share of ownership or special allocation as stated in the operating agreement. Ensuring the chosen method doesn't inadvertently trigger adverse tax treatment is essential, so consulting with a tax professional when crafting profit-sharing plans is wise.

In practice, many startup LLCs begin with simple ownership-based profit sharing to keep things manageable. As the business grows and changes, members might negotiate more complex arrangements tailored to efforts, investment levels, and future roles. Flexibility is one of the LLC's greatest strengths, but without clear agreements, that flexibility can quickly become a source of confusion and conflict. Regular communication and willingness to revisit profit allocations help ensure all members feel fairly treated and committed to the business's success.

For entrepreneurs planning to bring on new members or outside investors, having a well-defined profit allocation strategy upfront provides a professional foundation for negotiations. Investors want clarity on how profits are shared and assurance that the structure rewards performance and protects their stakes. Similarly, existing members benefit from knowing their income streams and roles won't be diluted unexpectedly. Thoughtful profit distribution puts your LLC in a stronger position to attract capital and talent while fostering a collaborative culture.

As an LLC owner, it's important to remember that profit allocation is not just about dividing money—it's a reflection of your company's values and priorities. Whether you choose equal splits, performance-based rewards, or preferred returns, the goal is to create a system that fuels motivation, aligns incentives, and supports sustainable growth. Successful profit distribution methods build trust among members, reduce conflict, and reinforce the financial discipline needed to maximize your LLC's potential.

In conclusion, the best method for allocating profits among LLC members depends on your company's unique composition, goals, and growth stage. Whether sticking to simple ownership percentages or adopting specialized allocations like guaranteed payments and preferred returns, the key is clarity and fairness. Craft your operating agreement to reflect these decisions explicitly, revisit your strategy periodically, and maintain open communication among members. Doing so will empower your LLC with a profit-sharing framework that motivates every participant and drives business success.

Tax Implications of Different LLC Profit Distribution Models

When it comes to distributing profits in an LLC, one of the most critical aspects to consider is how your chosen method affects taxation. LLCs enjoy a flexible structure that allows them to choose among various profit distribution models, but this flexibility comes with important tax consequences that can influence both your business's financial health and your personal tax obligations. Understanding these impacts helps ensure you maximize after-tax income while remaining compliant with IRS regulations.

The most common LLC profit distribution models include equal distributions based on ownership percentage, guaranteed payments to members, and special allocations. Each of these structures carries distinct tax implications depending on how the IRS views the nature of payments and the timing of income recognition. For entrepreneurs and small business owners aiming to grow their LLCs, grasping these differences is essential not only for efficiency but also for strategic tax planning.

Let's start by examining distributions based strictly on ownership percentages, which is the default approach when LLC members haven't agreed on anything special in their operating agreement. Income, losses, and deductions flow through to members in proportion to their ownership interests, meaning profits are generally allocated alongside the member's percentage stake. This method aligns closely with the concept of pass-through taxation, wherein the LLC itself usually does not pay federal income taxes. Instead, members receive Schedule K-1 forms reflecting their share of profits and report that income on their personal returns.

This pass-through approach can be advantageous because it avoids the double taxation commonly experienced by corporations, but it also means members are taxed on their distributive shares whether or not the LLC actually distributes those profits in cash. In other words, profits allocated on paper can trigger tax liabilities even if the cash remains within the company to support growth or cover expenses. This timing mismatch can challenge LLC owners who need to manage cash flow while meeting tax obligations.

Next, consider the use of guaranteed payments to members. Guaranteed payments function somewhat like salaries paid to LLC members for services rendered or capital invested, and they are treated differently for tax purposes. Unlike profit distributions, guaranteed payments are deductible business expenses for the LLC, reducing the company's overall taxable income. From the member's perspective, though, guaranteed payments are considered ordinary income and subject to self-employment taxes. This creates an immediate tax impact that needs careful budgeting, but it offers a predictable income stream to members.

The clear tax implication here is that guaranteed payments will reduce the business's net profits, lowering the pass-through income that members will report. This can work well for LLCs wanting to compensate members consistently while managing overall tax exposure, but it's important to plan ahead for the self-employment tax consequences that accompany guaranteed payments. Members receiving guaranteed payments can't avoid these taxes even if they also receive profit distributions later on.

Another important distribution model involves special allocations, where the LLC operating agreement specifies profit shares that differ from ownership percentages. This flexibility lets LLCs reward certain members with larger or smaller shares of profits to reflect their roles, contributions, or capital investments. The IRS permits special allocations, but they must have substantial economic effect—that means allocations must match the members' economic arrangements and intentions, not just be tax-driven schemes.

Special allocations can complicate tax filings because they require a clear rationale and thorough documentation to withstand IRS scrutiny. When done correctly, they allow the LLC to allocate tax burdens and benefits in ways that match members' expectations and business realities. For example, a member who provides more sweat equity might receive a larger share of profits, which means more taxable income passes to them on their K-1. This approach can incentivize active participation but also requires careful handling to avoid unintended tax liabilities.

It's crucial to recognize how state-level taxation interacts with these federal tax concepts. Some states impose additional taxes or fees on LLCs based on income, capital, or transaction levels, and profit distribution models may influence how much the LLC owes at the state level. Owners must stay aware of their LLC's state-specific tax environment to align distribution strategies with both federal and state obligations. Ignoring these nuances can result in unexpected tax bills or penalties.

Given the pass-through nature of LLC taxation, members pay taxes on their share of business income even if profits aren't distributed in cash. This structure often leads to so-called "phantom income," which can catch new LLC members off guard. For instance, a member might owe taxes on profits allocated to them but have no actual distributions to cover their tax bill. Recognizing this pitfall upfront encourages planning and communication among members to avoid cash shortages during tax season.

To mitigate phantom income issues, some LLCs structure profit distributions to align closely with tax allocations, distributing enough cash each year to cover tax liabilities. While this reduces tax surprises, it may constrain the LLC's ability to reinvest profits into growth opportunities. Balancing the needs of tax equity and business reinvestment is a challenge every LLC owner must face with prudence and flexibility.

Another factor impacting tax treatment is how losses are allocated. LLC members can generally use their share of business losses to offset other taxable income, subject to certain limitations. Loss allocations tied to profit distributions influence members' adjusted gross income and thus affect their overall tax picture. This interplay between profits, losses, and distributions means that profit distribution models don't just govern upside potential—they can also shape how the LLC weathers downturns and tax consequences arising from operating losses.

Entrepreneurs choosing between these models should consider how different allocations will impact their personal and business tax strategy. Consulting with tax advisors familiar with LLC structures is essential because small nuances in distribution plans can trigger significantly different tax outcomes. Being proactive ensures that the company and its members avoid surprises and leverage tax advantages wherever possible.

One often overlooked consideration is self-employment taxes. Passive investors in LLCs typically avoid these taxes on distributions but active members usually pay self-employment tax on their allocable share of business earnings. Profit distribution models that step up guaranteed payments or alter allocations may inadvertently increase self-employment tax exposure. Properly structuring distributions can optimize tax efficiency, but this usually requires professional guidance and a personalized approach reflecting the LLC's unique circumstances.

Finally, understanding how profit distribution methods affect estimated tax payments for LLC members is critical. Since members are taxed individually on their share of income, they must manage quarterly estimated tax payments carefully to avoid penalties. Different distribution models create variable income flows, potentially complicating members' personal tax planning. Keeping an eye on taxable income from the LLC ensures smooth cash management and helps maintain positive relationships among members.

In summary, the tax implications of various LLC profit distribution models are intricate and integral to successful financial management. Aligning your profit allocation approach with sound tax strategy empowers you to protect your business's resources while maximizing after-tax returns. It's a balancing act that demands intentional decision-making and often expert advice, but tackling it early strengthens your LLC's foundation and supports sustainable financial growth.

Chapter 9: Scaling Your LLC with Financial Discipline

Growing your LLC takes more than just ambition; it requires a steady grip on financial discipline that keeps expansion sustainable and controlled. Without careful planning and consistent oversight of your finances, rapid growth can quickly spiral into cash flow problems or unmanageable expenses. To scale effectively, you need to prioritize budgeting rigorously, monitor capital expenditures closely, and make strategic decisions grounded in realistic financial forecasts. This disciplined approach ensures you're not just chasing growth for growth's sake but building a business that can thrive long term without overextending itself. Keeping a clear focus on financial health while expanding will empower you to seize new opportunities confidently and maintain the stability necessary for ongoing success.

Planning for Sustainable Growth in LLC Finances

Growing an LLC is exciting, but it's easy to get carried away if financial planning isn't solid. Sustainable growth means expanding your business at a pace your finances can support without risking the long-term health of your company. This requires a clear strategy that balances ambition with caution, ensuring you don't overstretch cash flow or saddle your LLC with unnecessary debt.

First, it's important to recognize that sustainable growth hinges on maintaining a disciplined approach toward managing your resources.

This isn't just about cutting costs but about allocating capital wisely. Every dollar spent should contribute directly or indirectly to enhancing value, whether through investing in new products, hiring talent, or improving infrastructure. A thoughtful plan identifies growth drivers and focuses on those areas rather than spreading resources thin across too many fronts.

One practical step toward sustainability is building a rolling financial forecast that you revisit regularly. This forecast should include revenue projections, anticipated expenses, and cash flow trends. Doing this helps you spot potential shortfalls early and adjust your approach before financial strain becomes a problem. It also keeps your growth expectations tethered to reality, steering you away from overly optimistic targets that might encourage reckless spending.

Resisting the temptation to finance growth solely through outside capital is another crucial lesson. While loans or investor money can jump-start expansion, relying too heavily on external funds without a clear repayment or growth plan can put your LLC in a precarious position. Sustainable growth often involves reinvesting profits back into the business, allowing expansion to rest on a solid foundation of earned income instead of borrowed money.

Profit retention is a critical but often overlooked aspect of managing your LLC finances for growth. Early-stage companies may feel pressured to distribute profits to owners or members, but holding onto a portion of those profits provides a financial buffer. This reserve not only funds ongoing operations but also offers the flexibility to seize opportunities that arise unexpectedly. Think of it as a growth fund built from your own operational success rather than external contributions.

Another key piece is keeping your financial goals aligned with your business capacity. Growth that outpaces operational capability can lead to inefficiencies, customer service issues, or even reputational damage. Plan growth phases that match your ability to scale internal systems, from customer support to supply chain management. Sustainable financial planning takes a comprehensive view, understanding that every expansion piece needs supporting infrastructure.

Maintaining tight expense control is equally important during expansion. It doesn't mean cutting corners; instead, it means making sure every expense is justified in terms of how it drives value. Review your expenses regularly, focusing on reducing waste, negotiating better terms with vendors, and leveraging economies of scale when possible. Smart spending helps maintain healthy profit margins even while your business grows.

Tax planning should also be integrated into your growth strategy to avoid unpleasant surprises. Rapid growth can push your LLC into new tax brackets or subject it to additional state and local taxes. Work with an accountant familiar with LLC tax law to anticipate these changes and structure your finances accordingly, minimizing tax liabilities through proactive planning rather than reactive adjustments.

Don't underestimate the power of strong financial reporting during growth stages. Regular, detailed reports give you insight not just into what has happened, but also why. This allows quick detection of trends, enabling you to pivot if a particular growth initiative isn't delivering as expected. Transparency in financial data also builds trust with partners and lenders, which is crucial if outside financing becomes part of your plan.

In the process of scaling, it's tempting to chase new markets or product lines quickly, but sustainable growth demands patience and focus. Test new initiatives on a smaller scale before committing significant resources. Pilot projects provide valuable data and minimize the risk of costly mistakes. When you build success incrementally, your LLC can absorb shocks better and adapt faster.

Liquidity management takes on greater importance as your business grows. Short-term cash surpluses can turn into shortages if you're not careful, especially as payment cycles extend with new customers or suppliers. Having a clear grasp on cash flow timing ensures you don't find yourself stretched too thin between incoming and outgoing payments, which is often the point where profitable companies stumble.

Equally important is to revisit your growth goals regularly to confirm they're still realistic and aligned with your market conditions. Economic shifts, regulatory changes, or competitive threats can alter what's achievable. A flexible planning process helps you stay nimble while maintaining financial discipline, allowing adjustment without losing sight of long-term sustainability.

Successful scaling isn't just about increasing numbers; it's about building a business that can operate efficiently at every level. That means investing in staff training, improving operational processes, and upgrading your technology infrastructure as your LLC grows. These investments may seem like added expenses upfront, but they're necessary to sustain higher revenue volumes without proportional cost increases.

Creating sustainable growth plans also means setting clear financial guardrails. Define what levels of debt, cash reserves, and profitability ratios you're comfortable with and stick to them. These boundaries protect your LLC from overleveraging or running into cash crunches, which can stall or even reverse growth momentum.

Lastly, growth isn't purely a financial issue; it's about mindset too. Adopting a long-term perspective helps you prioritize stability over quick wins, and encourages strategies that build shareholder value over time. Sustainable growth is less glamorous than sudden leaps, but it lays the groundwork for a profitable, resilient business that can thrive well into the future.

Managing Expenses and Capital Expenditures During LLC Expansion

Expanding your LLC is an exciting phase, but it comes with its share of financial challenges. One of the key elements that can make or break this growth stage is how well you manage your expenses and capital expenditures. Growth demands investment, but without discipline, it can quickly turn into overspending. By carefully controlling both day-to-day expenses and larger, one-time purchases, you ensure that your LLC maintains financial health while scaling effectively.

When an LLC expands, expenses usually rise — sometimes dramatically. From hiring new staff and increasing marketing budgets to upgrading infrastructure, costs pile up quickly. However, it's important to distinguish between necessary growth-related expenses and unnecessary outlays that don't add value to your long-term strategy. Every dollar spent should be intentional, aligned with your broader financial goals, and justified by the impact it will have on future revenue or operational efficiency. This mindset encourages more thoughtful spending and guards against the common pitfall of unchecked costs during a phase of rapid change.

Budgeting for expansion is different than maintaining a steady-state budget. You're dealing with more variables, increased uncertainty, and sometimes larger-scale investments. It helps to break your expenses into categories — fixed, variable, and one-time capital expenditures — then set spending limits for each based on realistic forecasts and margin analyses. For instance, increasing office rent or payroll are fixed costs that require committed cash flow, whereas upgrading computer systems might be a capital expenditure that depreciates over several years. Understanding these distinctions is crucial to avoid liquidity crunches that can stall your progress.

Capital expenditures, or capex, deserve special attention in this phase. These are the significant outlays for assets like equipment, property, or technology that support future growth. Unlike regular expenses, capex tends to be large, infrequent, and capitalized on the balance sheet rather than immediately expensed. While investing in these assets is often necessary, it's vital not to let your enthusiasm for growth lead to overbuying or excessive borrowing. Conducting a rigorous return-on-investment analysis before committing to any major purchase will protect your LLC from burdensome debts and wasted resources.

Moreover, carefully timing your capital expenditures can improve cash flow management. For example, if your business can delay a non-critical equipment purchase until after a strong quarter, you'll preserve working capital for immediate needs like payroll and inventory. Alternatively, leasing equipment instead of outright purchasing can provide flexibility and reduce upfront expenses, though it may cost more over time. Exploring all financing and procurement options allows you to tailor your capital allocation to best fit your firm's unique financial profile.

Controlling operating expenses during expansion is equally important. It's easy to fall into the trap of assuming that increased sales justify proportional increases in overhead. However, without controls, expenses can outpace revenue growth and erode profitability. Implementing ongoing expense reviews will help keep spending aligned with your company's actual performance. Look closely at recurring costs such as subscriptions, vendor contracts, and utility bills, then negotiate or eliminate anything that no longer delivers value. Even small savings can accumulate to significant amounts, directly strengthening your cash position.

Another strategy involves leveraging economies of scale to your advantage. As your business grows, certain expenses per unit should ideally decrease. Bulk purchasing, improved supplier relationships, or the use of shared resources across departments can reduce costs over time. But it's crucial to validate that these efficiencies actually materialize. Track key financial ratios consistently, and compare them to industry benchmarks or previous periods. If your cost per unit isn't improving, or worse, rising, dig into the causes immediately and implement corrective measures before minor issues become systemic problems.

Technology investments play a vital role in managing expenses during expansion. Automating routine tasks such as invoicing, payroll, and inventory management not only saves time but also reduces errors and staffing costs. Cloud-based accounting and financial planning tools provide real-time visibility into your financial status, empowering you to make faster, data-driven decisions. While technology may require upfront capital spending, the long-term benefits in efficiency often outweigh initial costs. Just be mindful to choose scalable solutions that grow with your business so you avoid constant replacements or redundant systems.

One often overlooked aspect is training your team to be financially mindful. Employees who understand the financial impact of their decisions tend to be more resourceful and cost-conscious. Providing basic financial education or sharing budget goals can encourage a culture of discipline rather than entitlement. For example, staff who manage procurement or travel expenses should know the importance of adhering to spending limits. Creating clear policies and involving your team in financial responsibilities builds collective accountability that supports sustainable growth.

Growth also brings a greater need for careful documentation and oversight. Tracking expenses with precision allows you to analyze spending trends, identify cost overruns, and forecast future needs. Establishing systematic expense reporting and approval processes minimizes waste and fraud risk. Using budgets as living documents rather than static plans creates a continuous feedback loop: monitor your actual costs against projections and adjust quickly if deviations appear. This approach prevents surprises from suddenly draining your cash reserves.

Debt management intertwines closely with capital expenditures. While loans and lines of credit can fund necessary expansion investments, relying too heavily on borrowed money risks overleveraging your LLC. Before taking on new debt, examine interest rates, payment terms, and the impact on your monthly cash flow. It's wise to prioritize expenses that generate a clear return ahead of less urgent or speculative purchases. Maintaining a healthy balance between equity, retained earnings, and external financing ensures your business remains resilient during growth fluctuations.

Furthermore, timing plays a crucial role when paying vendors and managing payable terms. Negotiating favorable payment schedules can help smooth out cash flow peaks and valleys inherent in expansion. For example, extending payment terms without incurring penalties buys breathing room for your operational expenses, while seeking early payment discounts on key inputs lowers overall costs. Striking the right balance between honoring supplier relationships and optimizing your working capital is a skill that comes with experience but pays huge dividends in financial control.

Sometimes, scaling requires revamping your physical footprint—moving to a larger office, investing in distribution centers, or modifying retail venues. These capital expenditures are often visible signs of growth, yet without meticulous evaluation, they risk becoming financial burdens. Before committing, consider the location, long-term lease agreements, and potential for subleasing or exit options. Flexibility in physical assets can protect you in case the expansion does not proceed as planned and allow for easier adjustment without heavy penalties.

On the expense side, marketing and customer acquisition often ramp up with expansion goals. However, rather than just increasing budgets blindly, focus on measuring the return on these expenditures consistently. Digital marketing, for example, offers detailed data tracking, so you can identify which campaigns actually generate qualified leads or sales. Adjust strategies based on performance metrics to avoid wasting money on ineffective efforts. Remember, disciplined spending in marketing maximizes not just growth, but profitability as well.

When it comes to human resources, expanding your team is essential to support increased operations. Yet payroll is typically your largest fixed cost. Hiring decisions should align tightly with not just immediate needs but projected revenue growth as well. Consider leveraging part-time or contract workers to provide flexibility while limiting fixed payroll obligations. Additionally, investing in training current employees to take on broader responsibilities increases efficiency and delays the need for costly new hires.

Finally, adopting a mindset of continuous improvement in expense and capital expenditure management sets the stage for sustained success. Regularly revisiting your spending plans, capital investment priorities, and financing options keeps your LLC agile and resilient. Growth is never linear—unexpected challenges or opportunities arise frequently. If you maintain disciplined control over expenses and wisely allocate capital, you'll build a firm foundation that supports expansion without sacrificing financial stability.

Managing expenses and capital expenditures during LLC expansion is as much an art as it is a science. Staying vigilant, strategic, and flexible ensures you don't just grow bigger but grow stronger financially. This balance of ambition with discipline is critical to turning growth plans into lasting business success.

Chapter 10: Leveraging Technology for LLC Financial Management

In today's fast-paced business world, technology isn't just a convenience for LLC owners—it's a necessity that transforms how you manage your finances. Embracing the right financial tools and software can streamline bookkeeping, simplify budgeting, and give you real-time insights that empower smarter decisions. Automation helps reduce costly errors and frees up your time so you can focus on growth, not just spreadsheets. By integrating cloud-based platforms, mobile apps, and customized reporting systems, LLCs can maintain tighter control over cash flow and financial forecasting without the hassle of manual tracking. The right technology strengthens financial discipline and transparency, allowing you to confidently navigate the complexities of your business finances, operate more efficiently, and ultimately, scale with precision and agility.

Tools and Software Designed for LLC Financial Tracking

Successfully managing an LLC's finances often hinges on the ability to track income, expenses, and overall financial health consistently and accurately. Fortunately, the marketplace offers a wide range of financial tools and software specially designed to help LLC owners simplify this daunting task. These tools give business owners immediate access to vital financial data, organizing it in a way that's both intuitive and actionable. Whether you're working solo or managing a multi-member LLC, choosing the right financial software can transform the way you monitor your company's fiscal performance.

At its core, financial tracking software provides an organized framework for recording transactions, categorizing expenses, and monitoring cash flow. The days of juggling paper ledgers or using basic spreadsheets are long gone for anyone serious about business growth. Instead, smart software automates much of the bookkeeping process, reducing human error and freeing up time to focus on strategic decisions. Additionally, many tools come equipped with real-time dashboards, making it much easier to identify trends or flag potential issues before they escalate into bigger financial problems.

One of the biggest advantages of these digital tools is how they address the unique needs of LLCs, which often require tailored recordkeeping to respect member equity, capital contributions, and profit distributions. Unlike generic accounting solutions, several software options include features designed to manage these specific elements, ensuring compliance and transparency among members. This can be particularly valuable when you need to generate accurate financial reports for members or prepare for tax season. Having everything consolidated in one reliable platform minimizes the risk of misstatements or omissions that could complicate tax filings or internal audits.

The variety of software solutions available means you can select a platform aligned not only with your tracking requirements but also with your budget and technical capabilities. Cloud-based software has become extremely popular for LLC owners thanks to its accessibility from any device, scalability, and automatic updates that minimize IT headaches. Many tools offer mobile apps as well, so you can log expenses or check on your financial status on the go, an essential feature for busy entrepreneurs who don't stick to a desk. These conveniences help you stay on top of your finances no matter where your day takes you.

It's also worth noting that integration capabilities have become a major selling point. Financial tools that link directly to your bank accounts, payment processors, invoicing platforms, and even payroll services can streamline your entire financial workflow. This reduces the need for manual data entry and helps ensure your records are always current. The fewer systems you have to manage independently, the less likely errors will creep in, and the more comprehensive your financial overview becomes.

Choosing the right software starts with identifying the features that matter most for your LLC's operations. For some, basic bookkeeping combined with expense tracking might suffice; for others, more robust solutions offering budgeting tools, forecasting, inventory tracking, or multi-member accounting will be necessary. Many platforms provide tiered pricing plans, so you can start with what fits your needs and upgrade as your business grows. It's important to remember that spending a bit more upfront for a feature-rich tool can save hours of manual effort and stress in the long run.

Among the well-regarded financial tracking solutions for LLCs, certain names stand out because they blend user-friendly design with powerful functionalities. These tools often feature customizable reports and visual analytics, allowing you to see the story behind your numbers without digging through complex data sets. Some also provide industry-specific templates that take into account the unique accounting nuances relevant to your type of business. Finding software that 'speaks your language' reduces the learning curve and increases the likelihood you'll use it consistently.

Another important consideration is customer support and training resources offered by the software providers. LLC owners who aren't finance experts need clear guidance on navigating these tools effectively. Good software companies recognize this need and offer tutorials, webinars, live chat support, and community forums where business owners can share tips. When you feel confident using your financial software, you're more likely to maintain accurate records and spot warning signs early.

Security features shouldn't be overlooked either. Since your financial data is sensitive, choosing software with strong encryption, secure login protocols, and regular backups protects your business from data breaches or accidental loss. Many cloud-based platforms comply with industry standards for data security, giving LLC owners peace of mind. Before committing, it's wise to review the vendor's security policies and evaluate their track record for reliability and uptime.

Lastly, consider how implementing these tools fits within your broader financial management strategy. The best software doesn't just track numbers; it should empower you to make smarter decisions. When paired with sound financial knowledge, employing the right financial tracking tool positions your LLC for growth by enabling you to maintain a clear pulse on your company's fiscal landscape. Continuous, accurate tracking creates a foundation that supports budgeting, forecasting, tax preparation, and even discussions with investors or lenders.

To sum it up, integrating purpose-built financial tracking software into your LLC's operations is less about convenience and more about establishing effective discipline in managing money. These tools streamline tedious tasks and provide insights that would be nearly impossible to uncover manually. For LLC owners serious about driving long-term success, investing in the right technological solution is a step no one should overlook.

Automating Financial Processes to Save Time and Reduce Errors

Running an LLC means juggling a lot of moving parts, and your financial processes are no exception. The good news is that automation can dramatically lighten this load. By automating routine financial tasks, you free up valuable time that you can spend focusing on growth and strategy, rather than getting bogged down by repetitive data entry or manual calculations. More importantly, automation helps reduce costly errors that occur when human hands repeatedly handle complex financial information.

Consider the typical activities that form the backbone of your LLC's financial management—tracking expenses, invoicing clients, reconciling bank accounts, processing payroll, estimating taxes, and generating financial reports. Traditionally, many small business owners do these manually or rely on spreadsheets, which increases the risk of mistakes. Missed transactions, missed deadlines, and duplicated data entry can lead to inaccuracies that may disrupt cash flow or cause compliance headaches. When you automate these core processes, your LLC's financial health becomes more reliable, transparent, and easier to manage.

Automation tools and software have evolved to the point where they're accessible and cost-effective for most small businesses. You don't need to be a tech wizard to implement them either. Modern systems are designed with simplicity in mind, giving entrepreneurs intuitive interfaces and seamless integrations. This means your bookkeeping software can talk directly to your bank, your invoicing app can remind clients automatically, and your payroll solution can calculate taxes without you lifting a finger. When all these components work together, the risk of human error plummets because data moves smoothly from one stage to the next without manual intervention.

Time savings go beyond just reducing the hours spent crunching numbers. Automation also accelerates the entire financial workflow, shortening the lag between key tasks like recording expenses and reviewing financial statements. Faster access to updated financial information empowers you to make better, more informed decisions. Whether you're considering a new investment, planning your next marketing campaign, or adjusting your budget, having real-time data means less uncertainty and greater confidence.

Despite these obvious benefits, some entrepreneurs hesitate to embrace automation because of concerns about upfront costs or the complexity of setting up new systems. The reality is quite the opposite for many LLCs. Initial setup may require some attention, but most cloud-based financial tools are affordable and scalable as your business grows. More importantly, the time and money you save by reducing errors, avoiding late fees, shortening payment cycles, and eliminating redundant work can quickly offset those costs.

Another key advantage of automated financial processes is the improved accuracy they deliver, which increasingly matters as your LLC grows and your financial landscape becomes more complex. For example, automated expense tracking can categorize transactions correctly every time, ensuring your books stay clean and your tax filings are accurate. Payroll automation reduces the risk of miscalculating salaries or withholding taxes, helping you stay compliant with federal and state regulations. This not only protects your LLC from potential penalties but also nurtures trust with employees and stakeholders.

Automation also supports better audit readiness. Imagine having all your transactions recorded, categorized, and backed up consistently, with no missing data or manual errors to reconcile. This level of organization simplifies the work you'll need to provide your accountant or during an official audit. Financial transparency becomes a natural byproduct, enhancing your credibility when applying for loans or attracting investors. These stakeholders value accuracy and organization, making your LLC appear more professionally managed and financially sound.

Beyond traditional bookkeeping, modern automation innovations include the use of artificial intelligence (AI) and machine learning to flag unusual transactions or forecast cash flow issues before they become problematic. These proactive tools act as virtual advisors that keep an eye on your financial health around the clock. They catch red flags quickly, giving you more time to address issues before they escalate. For example, if your software detects a sharp spike in expenses related to a specific vendor, it can alert you instantly so you can investigate.

The benefits of automating payments and receivables deserve special mention. Automating vendor payments ensures bills are paid on time, avoiding late fees and strained supplier relationships. Meanwhile, automated invoicing and payment reminders encourage faster client payments, which improves your cash flow. Many systems also support multiple payment methods, letting customers pay through their preferred channels. This flexibility increases your chances of getting paid promptly each month.

Security is another important consideration when automating financial processes. Most reputable automation platforms use encryption and strict access controls to protect sensitive financial data. This level of security often exceeds what many small businesses can provide on their own, reducing risks related to data breaches or fraud. You'll still need to implement sound cybersecurity practices on your end—like using strong passwords and limiting access to sensitive information—but automation doesn't inherently increase risk when you choose trustworthy providers.

Transitioning from manual to automated processes can feel daunting, but it doesn't have to happen all at once. Start small by automating one or two financial tasks, such as expense tracking or invoicing. As you grow comfortable and see measurable benefits, gradually expand the scope. Many software options offer free trials or tiered pricing models, making it easy to test their effectiveness without committing upfront.

Finally, don't overlook the human element in all this technology. Automation tools don't replace the need for your financial oversight and strategy, but they enhance your ability to focus on them. By removing tedious tasks from your workload, you can spend more quality time analyzing financial data, developing growth strategies, building relationships with clients and vendors, and advancing your LLC's mission. The best outcome of automating financial processes isn't just saving time—it's freeing your energy to propel the business forward with greater confidence and efficiency.

In summary, automating financial processes for your LLC is a practical and powerful step toward running a smarter, more efficient business. It cuts down on errors, speeds up workflows, enhances compliance, improves cash flow management, and bolsters your financial intelligence. Embracing automation creates a solid foundation where your LLC can thrive financially without getting overwhelmed by operational complexity. The time saved and accuracy gained are investments that pay off quickly and keep your business on the path to sustained success.

Chapter 11: Preparing Your LLC for Economic Uncertainty

Economic uncertainty can strike unexpectedly, and the key to navigating it lies in proactive preparation rather than reactive measures. To safeguard your LLC through turbulent times, focus on creating robust cash reserves that provide a cushion when revenue dips or expenses surge. In parallel, developing clear contingency plans ensures you're ready to pivot business strategies swiftly without jeopardizing core operations. Maintaining financial discipline and continuously monitoring market indicators empower you to make informed adjustments that reduce vulnerabilities. By embedding resilience into your LLC's financial framework, you not only protect your business from shocks but also position it to seize opportunities when stability returns.

Building Cash Reserves and Contingency Plans for LLCs

One of the most critical steps in preparing your LLC for economic uncertainty is building a solid cash reserve. This financial cushion acts as a lifeline when unexpected expenses hit or when revenue dries up temporarily. Without a sufficient cash reserve, an LLC can quickly find itself struggling to cover payroll, rent, or essential operational costs. By setting aside funds regularly during profitable periods, you create a buffer that gives your business breathing room and protects it from the shocks of economic downturns.

Many LLC owners underestimate the importance of cash reserves, often viewing them as money that could be better spent on growth initiatives or marketing. However, having liquidity ready and accessible can actually enable growth. In tough times, businesses with cash reserves can seize opportunities to invest, negotiate better terms with suppliers, or pivot quickly without scrambling for emergency funds. Reserves aren't just about survival—they're about giving your LLC flexibility and resilience.

Start by setting a clear target for your cash reserve based on your business's monthly operating expenses. A common rule of thumb is to have between three and six months' worth of expenses saved. For LLCs in more volatile industries or those with irregular cash flow, aiming for six to twelve months can provide an even safer margin. This target should include all fixed costs like rent, utilities, insurance, and payroll. Knowing exactly how much you need helps focus your savings efforts and avoids the temptation to dip prematurely into reserve funds.

It's crucial that cash reserves remain liquid and easily accessible. Funds tied up in long-term investments or inventory won't be of much help during sudden economic shifts. Many LLCs keep their reserves in high-yield savings accounts or money market accounts that offer reasonable interest without sacrificing liquidity. The goal is to balance earning a return on your reserve funds with the ability to withdraw them quickly when necessary.

Building your cash reserve starts with disciplined budgeting. After covering your necessary expenses each month, commit a portion of your profits to this fund before allocating money to non-essential spending. Automating transfers into a reserve account each month can take the guesswork out of saving and reduce the risk of spending those funds elsewhere. Over time, even modest, consistent contributions can grow into a substantial safety net.

Alongside building your cash reserves, developing a robust contingency plan is vital. A contingency plan outlines how your LLC will respond to financial emergencies or unexpected disruptions. It goes hand in hand with your reserves by providing a roadmap for making smart decisions under pressure rather than reacting chaotically. Preparing this plan in advance empowers your LLC to act decisively and maintain stability in the face of uncertainty.

Your contingency plan should detail specific scenarios your LLC might face, such as sudden drops in sales, supplier interruptions, or economic recessions. For each, define the triggers that will activate your plan and the steps you'll implement to manage the situation. This might include cutting discretionary expenses, temporarily reducing staff hours, renegotiating payment terms with vendors, or shifting marketing focus to new customer segments. A clear, pre-established approach reduces downtime and financial risk when challenges arise.

Effective contingency planning also means identifying alternative sources of liquidity beyond your cash reserve. Building relationships with lenders before trouble hits can save valuable time if you suddenly need a loan. Keep lines of credit open and understand their terms fully, so you know exactly how much you can borrow and at what cost. Similarly, exploring partnerships or community support networks as part of your plan can offer non-financial resources that help sustain your business during tough periods.

Communication and documentation are key to making your contingency plan work smoothly. Make sure all LLC members and key employees understand the plan's components and their roles should a crisis occur. Document everything clearly in writing and review the plan regularly to keep it current with your evolving business environment. Economic uncertainty is not static; your responses must be adaptable and well-rehearsed to deliver maximum protection.

Another aspect often overlooked in both cash reserves and contingency plans is the psychological benefit they provide. Financial uncertainty can create stress and hesitation that paralyzes decision-making. Having a plan and reserve funds in place breeds confidence. This confidence enables you to navigate rough waters without panic, keeping your focus on strategic moves rather than just survival.

As you build your cash reserves, it's important to continue monitoring your overall financial health vigilantly. Reserves alone won't protect your LLC if underlying problems like poor cash flow management or unchecked expenses persist. Think of your cash reserve and contingency plan as parts of a larger ecosystem of financial discipline. They complement other systems like budgeting, forecasting, and tax planning to create a resilient, adaptable business.

Setting milestones in your cash reserve growth journey also helps maintain motivation and focus. Rather than fixate only on the final goal, celebrate when you hit increments—whether that's one month's expenses saved, or reaching the halfway mark. This progress tracking reinforces your commitment and keeps the entire team aligned around a shared financial safety goal.

In times of economic uncertainty, many LLC owners face difficult choices about whether to tap into their reserves early or hold fast. This decision should never be taken lightly. Lean on your contingency plan as a guide, and analyze carefully the cause and expected duration of the crisis before using reserve funds. Sometimes, a short-term disruption can be bridged with temporary cost-cutting without touching reserves. In more prolonged downturns, dipping into your reserve becomes necessary, but with a plan to replenish it as soon as conditions improve.

Ultimately, building cash reserves and contingency plans isn't just about surviving economic uncertainty. It's about thriving through it by giving your LLC a foundation of financial stability and strategic foresight. When unexpected storms come—and they will—your business will be prepared to weather them, emerge stronger, and keep moving toward growth and success.

Adapting Financial Strategies During Market Downturns

When the economy takes a hit, LLC owners face one of their toughest tests: keeping the business afloat without sacrificing long-term growth potential. Market downturns can range from brief recessions to prolonged slumps, and while no one can predict exactly how deep or long they'll last, smart entrepreneurs know that adaptability is key. Adapting your financial strategies during these periods isn't just about survival—it's about positioning your LLC to emerge stronger when conditions improve.

One of the first steps in responding to a downturn is gaining clear visibility into your financial standing. During stable periods, small cash flow gaps might fly under the radar, but in a contraction, every dollar counts. This means increasing the frequency and detail of your financial reviews—consider weekly or biweekly cash flow forecasts, budget reevaluations, and expense tracking. By having an up-to-date snapshot of your revenue inflows, outstanding obligations, and available liquidity, you'll be better equipped to make rapid decisions that keep your business grounded.

A critical shift often needed during downturns is recalibrating your budgeting mindset. Budgets that worked when demand was high or costs were steady may not hold up when sales slow down or supply chain expenses spike. Instead of clinging to previous figures, adopt a flexible budgeting approach that can be adjusted as new data emerges. This might mean temporarily cutting discretionary spending or postponing non-essential projects, but it's important the changes align with your core business objectives. You don't want to sell yourself short by trimming too deeply—focus on areas that deliver the most value or have the greatest impact on your customers.

Certain expenses will naturally come under scrutiny first, but be careful not to erode investments that maintain your business's competitive edge. For example, marketing budgets often face cuts, but strategic, lean marketing can help you retain customers and attract new ones even when budgets are tight. During downturns, it pays to get creative with low-cost or digital channels where returns are measurable and immediate. Meanwhile, operational efficiency should be optimized without compromising quality or service reliability. This often means renegotiating vendor contracts, seeking volume discounts, or exploring alternative suppliers to reduce costs.

Another essential tactic is managing your working capital more deliberately. During tough times, promptly collecting receivables and extending payables within reason can significantly boost your LLC's liquidity. Tightening credit policies on customer payments may seem harsh, but it can protect your cash flow and reduce bad debt risks. On the flip side, develop good communication with your own creditors and suppliers—explore payment plans or temporary extensions if needed. Many businesses discover that transparent conversations during downturns can lead to mutually beneficial agreements rather than rigid enforcement of terms.

The role of financial reserves cannot be overstated. If you've built a cash cushion ahead of time, it's your LLC's shock absorber during market volatility. These reserves provide the flexibility to cover core expenses without scrambling for emergency funding. If you haven't prioritized reserves yet, focus on establishing at least a modest emergency fund as soon as possible. Start small if needed, setting aside even a fraction of monthly revenue to build momentum. The peace of mind and operational continuity these reserves offer make all the sacrifices worthwhile.

In some cases, downturns present opportunities rather than just threats. For LLC owners with cash reserves or access to affordable financing, economic uncertainty can be the right time to invest in areas your competitors might neglect. Whether it's acquiring discounted equipment, investing in staff training, or improving technology infrastructure, bold moves made prudently during downturns can pay dividends when growth resumes. The challenge lies in balancing risk—aggressive spending is dangerous without a clear financial plan, but complete retrenchment might cause you to miss a window of advantage.

Speaking of financing, reconsider your capital structure during downturns. If your LLC depends heavily on debt, review existing loan arrangements and explore refinancing options. Lower interest rates or extended payment terms can ease immediate cash flow pressure. Similarly, if equity investment is part of your growth story, market conditions may affect valuation and investor appetite. Although it might be tempting to delay seeking funding, sometimes preparing for and pursuing capital during a downturn can strengthen your LLC's prospects for survival and expansion. Present realistic, updated financial projections to potential lenders or investors to reflect current challenges transparently.

It's also important to keep an eye on your pricing strategies during trouble times. Maintaining pricing levels might be essential to protect your margins, but rigid pricing can drive away price-sensitive customers. Consider introducing flexible pricing models such as discounts on volume purchases, extended payment deadlines, or bundled services. These approaches can stimulate demand while preserving relationships. However, communicate any changes clearly and consistently to avoid confusion or perceived loss of value.

Personnel costs typically represent a large portion of an LLC's expenses. When revenue dips, decisions around staffing become difficult but unavoidable for many. Instead of resorting to layoffs immediately, explore alternative strategies like reduced hours, temporary furloughs, or role realignments to spread the financial impact without losing valuable talent. LLC owners should also consider cross-training employees to cover essential functions efficiently, a move that increases resilience without increasing headcount. Transparent communication with your team about challenges and plans fosters loyalty and cooperation, which are invaluable during uncertain times.

Another dimension of adapting during downturns is strengthening your financial forecasting and scenario planning. Traditional static budgets won't cut it when market conditions fluctuate rapidly. Develop multiple scenarios ranging from optimistic to worst-case and prepare corresponding financial responses. This method enhances your ability to pivot quickly if assumptions change. Moreover, detailed scenario analyses provide the confidence to make tough calls because you've already anticipated potential outcomes, reducing the paralysis that uncertainty can trigger.

Beyond internal controls, staying informed about macroeconomic indicators and industry trends will give you early clues about how and when to adjust strategies. Linking your financial management to external data such as interest rates, unemployment figures, or consumer confidence indexes adds an extra layer of insight. Engaging with peers in your industry or professional networks can also reveal best practices and innovative survival strategies tailored to your market.

Finally, mindset plays a crucial role in navigating financial turbulence. Downturns test not only your LLC's fiscal health but also your resolve as an owner. Maintaining a positive, proactive attitude helps you approach challenges as strategic puzzles to solve rather than uncontrollable disasters. Successful entrepreneurs use these periods to build financial discipline, streamline operations, and foster a culture of resilience within their LLCs. Each downturn survived proves a stepping stone toward sustainable success.

Adapting financial strategies during market downturns calls for a blend of discipline, flexibility, and foresight. The goal isn't to play it safe by freezing all activity but to adjust deliberately and thoughtfully, balancing short-term cash preservation with investments that ensure your LLC's future. By continuously monitoring your finances, optimizing expenses, leveraging opportunities, and preparing for multiple scenarios, your LLC can not only weather economic uncertainty but emerge stronger and more competitive.

Chapter 12: Exit Strategies and Succession Planning for LLCs

Planning ahead for an exit or succession is essential for any LLC owner focused on securing lasting financial success and legacy. Whether you're considering selling your LLC, transferring ownership to family, or bringing in a new generation of leadership, having a clear strategy ensures a smooth transition without sacrificing the value you've built. It's about more than just timing the market or finding the right buyer; it requires understanding the financial implications, preparing your business for transfer, and aligning your personal and professional goals. Effective exit and succession planning empowers you to protect your investment, maintain business continuity, and achieve peace of mind knowing your LLC will continue to thrive long after you step back. Start this process early—because without a solid plan, even the most profitable LLC can face unnecessary risks and missed opportunities.

Financial Considerations When Selling or Transferring an LLC

When it comes time to either sell or transfer your LLC, understanding the financial implications is crucial. Handing over ownership involves far more than just signing on the dotted line. The financial landscape around such transactions can be complex, and overlooking even one element might seriously impact your bottom line or the future of your business. Whether you're looking to cash out, bring in a new partner, or transition your LLC to family members or employees, having a keen sense of the financial terrain will empower you to make decisions that protect your interests and maximize value.

The first consideration in any sale or transfer is valuing the LLC accurately. This isn't just about putting a price tag on your business, but conducting a thorough valuation that accounts for assets, liabilities, market position, cash flow, and future earning potential. Entrepreneurs often get emotional and either undervalue or overestimate what their business is worth, both of which can have negative consequences. Employing professional appraisers or financial analysts can provide an objective valuation that buyers or transferees will respect and that holds up during negotiations. This careful assessment lays the groundwork for a financial win-win or at least a clear, defensible starting point.

Understand that the structure of the transaction impacts your taxes and cash flow. Are you selling membership interests or the company's assets? The difference can greatly affect the tax treatment. A membership interest sale typically triggers capital gains tax, calculated on the difference between your basis in the interests and the sale price. Asset sales, on the other hand, might generate a more complex tax picture involving depreciation recapture and different rates for various types of assets. Before committing, walk through these scenarios with a qualified tax advisor who can map out what your real tax liability will look like post-transaction.

Equally important is considering outstanding liabilities and debts in the financial analysis. Your LLC may have loans, unpaid invoices, pending legal obligations, or other debts that could either be transferred to a new owner or need to be settled before closing. Buyers will factor this into their offer, often reducing it to hedge their risk. From your side, negotiating who assumes which liabilities needs crystal clarity in the sale agreement. Leaving any ambiguity might expose you to financial liabilities after the sale or derail the transaction if the buyer feels uncertain about the risk they're taking on.

Cash flow history plays a pivotal role in how your LLC is perceived financially. Prospective buyers or transferees want to see stable or growing cash flow patterns because that's the clearest indicator of ongoing profitability. It's your job to provide clean, detailed financial records that show this history. If your cash flow fluctuates wildly, consider what financial controls or operational strategies you can implement now to make your LLC's future look more reliable. A business with robust, predictable cash flow attracts higher offers and easier financing, which benefits everyone involved in the exit process.

When preparing to sell or transfer your LLC, it's also essential to consider the timing from a financial standpoint. Market conditions, industry cycles, and the economic environment can significantly influence your LLC's value. For example, selling during a downturn may mean accepting a lower price, while waiting for an upswing could increase your returns. Look at industry trends, competitor sales, and broader economic indicators to choose a window that maximizes your financial advantage. Sometimes, even a few months' patience might translate to tens of thousands or more in additional proceeds.

One often overlooked factor is the cost of the transfer itself. Closing costs, legal fees, broker commissions, and due diligence expenses can add up quickly and eat into your net proceeds. Budget carefully for these expenses as part of your exit planning. Think of these outflows as investments in achieving a clean, smooth transition that avoids future disputes or complications. Sometimes paying for experienced professionals upfront saves much more money down the road by preventing errors or renegotiations.

For LLC owners contemplating transferring the business to family members or employees, gift and estate tax implications must be carefully examined. Gifting membership interests may trigger tax events for both the giver and the receiver, especially if done without professional planning. Succession strategies that include financial gifting require a nuanced approach to minimize tax exposure while ensuring the business remains financially viable. Those considering employee stock ownership plans (ESOPs) or other incentive-based transfers should understand the funding requirements and ongoing financial obligations such structures can impose on the LLC.

Another key financial aspect is how you handle existing contracts, leases, and customer relationships during the sale or transfer. The stability and longevity of these agreements influence the valuation and future cash flow projections. Buyers often scrutinize these contracts for potential liabilities or opportunities, which can affect how much they're willing to pay or what conditions they set. It pays to organize and possibly renegotiate key contracts ahead of time to strengthen your LLC's financial position and make the transition smoother. Remember, a buyer isn't just purchasing assets—they're acquiring a going concern.

Addressing outstanding financial obligations also extends to member loans or capital accounts. If you or other members have loaned money to the LLC or contributed capital expecting returns, these figures must be settled or clearly accounted for before ownership changes hands. The more clarity and fairness achieved here, the less likely disputes become a roadblock in closing the deal. Equitable treatment ensures that the financial framework supporting the business remains solid, which benefits incoming owners and your legacy simultaneously.

It's tempting to speed through paperwork and contracts, but every word can have financial consequences. Detailed buy-sell agreements and transfer documents need to be crafted with care to reflect payment terms, indemnifications, representations, warranties, and contingency plans. These provisions manage risk and provide financial protections that can prevent costly battles later. Investing time and resources into this documentation pays dividends by reducing uncertainty and preserving the value you've worked hard to build.

Liquidity after the sale or transfer is another critical financial consideration. Will you receive a lump sum, structured payments, or a profit-sharing arrangement? Each option affects your cash flow and tax profile differently. Structured payments or earnouts can help secure higher overall returns if the business performs well post-transfer but also carry risks that future income may be less than expected. Assess your personal financial needs and risk tolerance before agreeing to complex payment structures. If possible, negotiate terms that provide a safety net or milestones that release payments based on performance.

Finally, as you move through the process, keep in mind that transparency, communication, and realistic expectations make all the difference. Buyers, transferees, and financial advisors all appreciate clear, accurate financial information delivered professionally. Preparing your LLC financially for sale or transfer isn't just about numbers; it's about building trust that the business is a sound investment. When everyone involved understands the financial picture, negotiations tend to be smoother, and outcomes more favorable.

In short, managing the financial considerations when selling or transferring your LLC is a multi-faceted challenge that demands planning, knowledge, and expert support. Approach the process methodically and avoid rushing decisions. By evaluating valuation, tax implications, liabilities, contracts, costs, payment structures, and timing with an informed eye, you position your LLC—and yourself—for a financially successful transition. This kind of thoughtful preparation not only secures your financial future but also helps empower the next owner to take your business to new heights.

Planning for Long-Term Legacy and Continuity in LLC Ownership

When you think about your LLC, it's natural to focus on day-to-day operations, growth, and immediate financial goals. However, a truly successful business owner looks beyond those horizons. Planning for long-term legacy and continuity isn't just about what happens when you exit; it's about ensuring your LLC can thrive well into the future, regardless of changes in ownership or management. This forward-thinking approach secures the value you've built and protects both your family's and your business's financial futures.

Legacy planning begins with a clear understanding of what you want your business to represent years down the line. Is your LLC designed to stay within the family, pass to key employees, or be sold to an outside party? Each choice carries unique considerations that affect how you structure ownership, control, and financial arrangements today. The goal is to establish a framework that supports your vision while offering flexibility when life inevitably throws curveballs your way.

Continuity planning often involves creating strategies to manage transitions smoothly and keep the LLC operational, even if founding members step away due to retirement, illness, or other reasons. Without solid plans, unexpected shifts in leadership or ownership can destabilize your business, erode value, and create costly disputes among members. You'll want to avoid that scenario by putting mechanisms in place well before any changes arise.

One critical aspect of long-term planning is defining clear ownership structures and membership agreements that anticipate potential future scenarios. These documents act like instruction manuals for handling changes in ownership, whether it's through voluntary transfers, inheritance, or forced sales. When ownership rights and responsibilities are spelled out in detail, they help minimize confusion and conflict, preserving relationships and the business's health.

It's also wise to regularly review and update these agreements to reflect any shifts in your business's goals or member circumstances. Life changes fast—people's priorities shift, markets evolve, and new opportunities or threats emerge. Staying proactive makes sure that planning doesn't get stuck in the past but instead matches your present-day realities and ambitions.

Financially, building a legacy requires balancing growth with sustainability. That means reinvesting earnings in ways that boost long-term resilience rather than chasing quick wins that may jeopardize stability. Establishing reserves or funds dedicated to succession and estate planning can provide a cushion for transitions, helping to avoid financial strain when ownership changes hands. These reserves could also pay for legal fees or taxes related to transfers, easing burdens on successors.

Another vital part of continuity involves preparing successors—whether family members, trusted employees, or partners—to step into leadership roles confidently. This preparation is more than just handing over the keys; it's about mentoring, training, and gradually transferring knowledge and responsibility. A well-prepared successor will honor your legacy by maintaining established financial practices and nurturing the company culture that made your LLC successful.

Incorporating professional advisors into your planning process can make a big difference. Estate planners, financial consultants, and legal experts bring perspectives that help anticipate challenges and identify opportunities you might miss on your own. These professionals can guide you on tax-efficient ownership transfer methods, liability protections, and setting up trusts or buy-sell agreements—all tools that contribute to stable and lasting business continuity.

Trust and buy-sell agreements deserve special attention because they establish rules for if and when ownership interests change hands. These agreements can dictate who gets the option to buy a departing member's share, at what price, and under what conditions—preventing unwanted owners or external parties from gaining control. Carefully crafted, these provisions foster alignment among members and create predictable outcomes that protect everyone involved.

While setting up these structures, remember the importance of communication. Transparent conversations among members encourage trust and shared commitment to the long-term success of the LLC. It's natural to avoid difficult topics like death or disability planning, but confronting them head-on is exactly what shields your business from chaos in tough times. Holding regular planning meetings can keep everyone on the same page and adjustments responsive to new developments.

With today's technological tools, capturing and sharing critical business knowledge has become simpler, which supports continuity in profound ways. Documenting key processes, financial controls, client relationships, and supplier arrangements ensures your LLC's day-to-day operations aren't overly dependent on any one person. This institutional knowledge acts as a safeguard, empowering successors to keep the wheels turning smoothly.

Finally, remember that long-term legacy planning isn't a one-time project but a living process. As your LLC evolves, revisit your plans and legacy goals regularly. Economic conditions shift, tax laws change, and personal priorities can transform alongside business growth. Staying engaged with your legacy and succession plan keeps your LLC adaptable and ready to face whatever the future holds.

Your LLC is more than a business—it's a reflection of your hard work, values, and aspirations. By investing time and effort into thoughtful long-term planning, you're building a foundation that extends well beyond your involvement. Not only can this planning protect your financial interests, but it also ensures that the journey you've started can inspire and sustain others who come after you.

Chapter 13: Empowering LLC Owners to Master Their Financial Future

As we reach the culmination of this guide, it's clear that mastering the financial aspects of running an LLC is much more than just crunching numbers — it's about mindset, discipline, and a proactive approach. Financial success for your LLC doesn't happen by accident. It requires consistent effort, informed decision-making, and a willingness to adapt to changing circumstances. By now, you've seen how foundational principles and practical strategies weave together to shape a resilient business that not only survives but thrives.

The central theme throughout this journey is empowerment. You're not just managing an LLC; you're taking control of an intricate financial ecosystem. This ecosystem involves setting clear goals, maintaining precise records, effectively managing cash flow, understanding tax obligations, and deploying smart growth tactics. When these elements sync up, they offer you a distinct advantage: the ability to anticipate challenges, seize opportunities, and confidently steer your business toward long-term prosperity.

One of the most powerful takeaways from this guide is the importance of financial literacy tailored specifically for LLCs. Unlike generic business models, LLCs have unique tax structures, legal frameworks, and operational nuances. Understanding these sets you apart from those who simply run their companies "on the fly." You're equipped with a deeper insight that enables better decision-making and strategic planning.

If there's one thing to remember, it's this: financial mastery is a continuous process. It's never a one-and-done deal. Markets shift, tax laws evolve, and your business grows in ways that require you to revisit your strategies regularly. Being flexible and open to learning will keep your LLC agile and ready to adapt. Staying engaged with your financial management, rather than outsourcing it blindly, gives you the power to catch issues early and capitalize on favorable moments.

Running an LLC successfully means balancing the practicalities of daily operations with the vision for where you want your business to go. This balance is often the biggest challenge for entrepreneurs. You've learned how to develop a reliable budget system designed specifically to fit an LLC's cash flow needs and expenses. Budgeting isn't about limiting spending — it's about prioritizing what moves your business forward and cutting out fiscal guesswork.

Cash flow management, another pillar of financial health, is where many LLC owners stumble if they're unprepared. But once you master the art of tracking, forecasting, and adjusting your inflows and outflows in real time, you can avoid the cash crunches that often derail growth. That proactive stance lets you strategically reinvest profits or shore up reserves for slower months without panic.

Tax responsibilities can feel daunting, but knowledge is your best defense. Federal and state requirements for LLCs carry nuances that can either cost you or save you plenty, depending on how well you navigate them. Finding legitimate deductions and credits, keeping your filings accurate, and understanding the timing involved will help prevent surprises come tax season. Financial mastery means treating taxes not as a dreaded chore, but as a core part of your financial strategy.

Growth doesn't just happen—it's a deliberate act that requires careful investment and risk management. Knowing when and where to allocate resources without jeopardizing your core operations is crucial. Smart investment planning should align with your overall business goals, supporting sustainable expansion rather than chasing quick wins that might leave you vulnerable. Along with that, protecting your business through insurance and legal safeguards ensures that unexpected setbacks won't derail everything you've built.

When it comes to funding, understanding your options lets you choose the path that best fits your LLC's stage and objectives. Whether it's traditional loans, investor capital, or alternative financing, preparation is key. Pitching your LLC to lenders or investors with clear financials and a convincing plan improves your chances of securing the resources you need to grow thoughtfully and on your terms.

Accurate and timely financial records form the backbone of all wise decisions. From tax filings to profit allocations, having clean data instills confidence and gives you a snapshot of your company's health at any moment. This organization also empowers you to scale your operations without losing control over costs or quality. Scaling with discipline means anticipating future expenses and capital needs before they become urgent problems.

Technology offers a tremendous edge in managing these complex tasks. Choosing the right tools and automating routine financial processes can save you valuable time, reduce mistakes, and provide real-time insights. Embracing these innovations helps simplify your workload and frees you up to focus on the bigger picture of your LLC's development.

Finally, no financial journey is complete without preparing for uncertainties and planning your eventual exit or succession. Building cash reserves and contingency plans creates a safety net that will support your business through economic downturns or unforeseen crises. And thoughtful exit strategies guarantee your personal legacy and the future success of your LLC, whether that means selling, passing it on, or restructuring ownership.

Taking all these elements together, your role as an LLC owner is not just to manage finances but to harness them as a powerful tool that fuels your vision. The financial confidence you cultivate opens doors—to new markets, better partnerships, and opportunities you might never have imagined. It also gives you peace of mind, knowing you can meet challenges head-on and maintain control over your company's destiny.

Financial mastery is a journey worth committing to because it's the foundation upon which your entrepreneurial dreams stand. Each dollar tracked, every strategy implemented, and all knowledge gained reinforce your ability to build a thriving LLC. Let this be your call to action: keep learning, stay organized, think strategically, and remember that your financial future is something you command—not something that simply happens to you.

With determination and the right tools, your LLC's financial success isn't just a goal—it's an attainable reality. Empower yourself with these insights and move forward with confidence, knowing you have what it takes to master your financial future and create the lasting business impact you envision.

Appendix A: Additional Resources for LLC Financial Success

Running an LLC comes with plenty of financial challenges and opportunities. While this book provides a solid framework for managing your LLC's finances, having access to additional resources can make a big difference in your success. Below is a curated list of tools, websites, books, and organizations that can support you on your financial journey.

Online Tools and Software

- **Accounting Software:** Tools like QuickBooks, Xero, and FreshBooks are designed to simplify bookkeeping and financial tracking. They help you stay organized and generate accurate reports without needing advanced accounting skills.
- **Budgeting and Cash Flow Apps:** Applications such as Float and Pulse give real-time insights into cash flow, allowing you to forecast needs and avoid surprises in your operating capital.
- **Tax Solutions:** Services like TurboTax Self-Employed and TaxAct specialize in handling the complexities of LLC taxes, ensuring you claim all appropriate deductions and stay compliant with state and federal rules.

Educational Websites and Online Communities

- **SBA.gov (U.S. Small Business Administration):** Offers excellent guidance on financial planning, funding options, and government resources tailored specifically for small businesses and LLCs.
- **IRS.gov:** The IRS website has dedicated sections for LLC taxation with detailed instructions, forms, and updates crucial for keeping your tax obligations on track.
- **Score.org:** Connect with volunteer business mentors who provide free advice, workshops, and downloadable templates focused on financial management for LLCs.
- **LinkedIn Groups and Reddit:** Join business-oriented groups and forums where LLC owners share firsthand experiences, strategies, and helpful resources.

Recommended Books for Deeper Learning

- **"Financial Intelligence for Entrepreneurs" by Karen Berman and Joe Knight:** A great primer to better understand financial statements and how they relate to your business decisions.
- **"The E-Myth Revisited" by Michael E. Gerber:** Offers insights into building a business with systems that include financial discipline at every level.
- **"Profit First" by Mike Michalowicz:** Challenges traditional accounting habits and introduces a system that helps businesses prioritize profit from day one.

Professional Services and Support

- **Certified Public Accountants (CPAs):** Finding a CPA who understands LLC structures can save you money and headaches by optimizing your tax position and ensuring regulatory compliance.

- **Financial Advisors:** An advisor familiar with small business finance can assist with investment planning, risk management, and growth strategies tailored to your LLC's unique circumstances.
- **Business Attorneys:** For risk mitigation and succession planning, consulting with a lawyer experienced in LLCs can protect your assets and clarify complex financial provisions.

Incorporating trusted resources like these into your routine can complement the financial strategies you implement for your LLC. They provide a knowledge base that keeps you informed, tools that streamline your workflows, and professional guidance when facing complex decisions. The more you leverage these supports, the stronger your LLC's financial foundation will become.

Consistent learning and utilizing quality resources empower you to make smarter decisions and confidently steer your business toward long-term financial success.

www.ingramcontent.com/pod-product-compliance
Lightning Source LLC
LaVergne TN
LVHW100326210926
848480LV00003B/1269